ARUN K. TIWARI

PRABHAT
PRAKASHAN

Published by
PRABHAT PRAKASHAN PVT. LTD.
4/19 Asaf Ali Road,
New Delhi-110 002 (INDIA)
e-mail: prabhatbooks@gmail.com

ISBN 978-93-5521-788-2
SOCRATES: A COMPLETE BIOGRAPHY
by Arun K. Tiwari

Edition
2025

Price
₹ 350 (Rupees Three Hundred Fifty only)

Printed at
R-Tech Offset Printers, Delhi

Dr. A P J Abdul Kalam

10, Rajaji Marg,
New Delhi-110 011
www.abdulkalam.com

Foreword

I visited Greece in 2007. When I was in Athens, I requested my hosts to take me to the prison cave, where Socrates drank the cup of poison. My request was met with hesitation but eventually they agreed. After a long uphill walk in Acropolis, I arrived at the Socrates Cave. Though we were a large group, I requested to be left alone for sometime in the Cave. It was dark inside except for a temporary light put in for my unscheduled visit.

All the people in my group very graciously stayed away. When I was alone, a very strong silence enveloped me. In the inner space of mind some thoughts arrived, as if from a very distant place.

"You are coming from the great democratic land of India. Kalam, do you know that it is in this great land that democracy was born? Great thinkers spread over several generations developed democratic concepts and refined the governance of the people by the people." I asked, "O Socrates, why did you sacrifice your life? Why?" I heard an echo. "Without sacrifice, no great thoughts would have possibly transformed into action. I had to give my life to the world for freedom of thoughts. Kalam tell the Indian youth to know their thoughts, refine their thoughts, live by their thoughts and struggle for the freedom of their thoughts."

Socrates had an early interest in the scientific theories of Anaxagoras, who taught that there are an infinite number of different kinds of elementary particles (atoms) and it is the action of Mind upon these that produces the objects that we see. Socrates believed that the senses of the body created difficulty for the thinking of the mind and came to regard the physical world as deceptive.

He believed that his work, which he sought to understand through critical questioning and dialogue, was given to him as a divine mission and, hence, was his duty. His total lack of interest in material possessions was evident by his always being barefoot and wearing an old cloak the whole year round. His habit of going barefoot even in winter showed his powers of endurance too. To him, the aspiration for virtue was the highest aim anyone could have.

On refusing to compromise on his principles or disobey the law, Socrates was brought to the Athenian court, at the age of 71. He was charged for being an evil doer, wrongfully teaching false doctrines to young people, being greedy and charging exorbitant sums of money for his teaching, besides being an atheist and denying belief in the Greek gods. Although he was sentenced to death, according to Athenian procedure, he could have appealed and probably would have received a lesser sentence. But he refused to appeal and drank the prescribed hemlock.

Socrates left no writings of his own, but his best known disciples, Plato and Xenophon, wrote exhaustively, not only giving accounts of the discussions Socrates held in Athens, but also incorporating Socrates' own beliefs. Three of Plato's dialogues, Apology, Crito and Phaedo, and Xenophon's Memorabilia are included in this book as Chapters.

Socrates' philosophy was a matter of how to live one's life. In subsequent centuries the love of wisdom became a great deal more academic, something that could be as remote from people's practical concerns as a game of chess. "There are nowadays professors of philosophy, but not philosophers", Thoreau writes in Walden. And he adds, "To be a philosopher is to love wisdom as to live according to its dictates, it is to solve some of the problems of life, not only theoretically, but practically."

Arun has worked on many books with me. He is candid and eloquent in putting across the life and times of Socrates for the readers not much familiar with the Greek history. He has placed Socrates' thoughts in the modern perspective. It is my hope that this book will help readers to be virtuous and apply Socratic ideas to situations in their own lives and seek meaning out of the otherwise unproductive and uninspiring life.

(A.P.J. Abdul Kalam)

27 March, 2009

Author's Note

Motivating Thoughts of Socrates

- By all means marry; if you get a good wife, you'll be happy. If you get a bad one, you'll become a philosopher.
- Death may be the greatest of all human blessings.
- Do not do to others what angers you if done to you by others.

Socrates's life has been known by the works of his pupils Plato and Xenophon, and Aristophanes's plays. It is impossible to establish the veracity of the matter regarding his life, but after putting different accounts together by the help of these sources, one can at least make some claims. He was thought to have been born circa 470 BC in Athens, Greece to Sophroniscus, an Athenian stone mason and sculptor, and Phaenarete, a midwife.

Socrates belonged to the lower class and due to that he did not receive extraordinary education like Plato and Aristotle did. He also learned the art of masonry from his father, and struggled as a mason for many years. The ways in which he became inclined towards philosophy still remains an unknown fact. Both Xenophon and Aristophanes claim that he received payment for teaching, while Plato disagrees that he did not receive payments, which led to his deprived condition.

He tied the martial knot with a much younger woman, Xanthippe, whom Xenophon labels as 'undesirable' as she was unhappy with Socrates' inability to make end meet as a philosopher. Socrates and Xanthippe had three sons—Lamprocles, Sophroniscus and Menexenus, but he was not involved with his children, and was more caught up in the intellectual evolution of the young boys of Athens.

It is presumed that he served in the armored infantry, was a part of three military campaigns during the Peloponnesian War, and was recognised for his valour.

Not much is known about Socrates's physical appearance, but Plato's Symposium attempts to capture him, as the unconventional male, who was short and stout, and had extraordinarily big eyes.

Athens was the experimentative space for him like a classroom but he didn't profess about what he knew. He used the method of ignorance to ask questions in a dialectic method, known as the Socratic Method, which forced the people to think. He insisted upon the greater importance of the mind, and is remembered for his challenging approach to Greek conventional wisdom.

Socrates was directly affected by the period of political Athenian instability and was put on trial, wherein the judges were not convinced by the defense of Socrates, possibly due to the vehement tone of his defense. He was eventually convicted by a vote-margin of 280 to 221. He was himself responsible in making things worse regarding the right and apt punishment for him. He could have chosen to be exiled, but asked to be rewarded and paid remuneration for his efforts in enlightening the city and its inhabitants. Naturally the displeased jury sentenced him to death by making him consume poison hemlock. His friends and followers tried to bribe the guards and wriggle him out of the punishment by making him to exile himself, but he refused the offer stating that death did not scare him, and he was a loyal denizen of Athens. Socrates's execution is described by Plato in his Phaedo dialogue: 'Socrates drank the hemlock mixture without hesitation. Numbness slowly crept into his body until it reached his heart. Shortly before his final breath, Socrates described his death as a release of the soul from the body.'

Socrates, one of the finest philosophers that the world could have, always emphasized the importance of the mind over the relative unimportance of the human body. This work is an effort to remember the credos, the adages, and the statements which Socrates left behind. Surely, his unconventional and iconoclastic ideas are going to also incite the readers of this book too to think and interrogate.

Acknowledgements

I gratefully acknowledge my teachers Dr. A.P.J. Abdul Kalam, Dr. B. Soma Raju and Dr. P. Krishnam Raju who helped me know myself in their own different ways.

I am thankful to my wife Dr. Anjana Tiwari who took me to Greece for 7th Hellenic Congress of Clinical Chemistry held in Athens, 16-19 October 2008.

A Brief Biography: Socrates

Socrates was born circa 469-70 BC in Athens, Greece. He was a philosopher and is considered the father of western philosophy. Plato was his most famous student and would teach Aristotle who would then tutor Alexander the Great. By this progression, Greek philosophy, as first developed by Socrates, was spread throughout the known world during Alexander's conquests.

He studied music, gymnastics, and grammar in his youth (the common subjects of study for a young Greek) and followed his father's profession as a sculptor. Tradition holds that he was an exceptional artist, and his statue of the Graces, on the road to the Acropolis, is said to have been admired into the 2nd century CE. Socrates served with distinction in the army and, at the Battle of Potidaea, saved the life of General Alcibiades.

We know of his life through the writings of his students, including Plato and Xenophon. When the political climate of Greece turned, Socrates was sentenced to death by hemlock poisoning in 399 BC. He accepted this judgment rather than fleeing into exile.

Early Years

Born circa 470 BC in Athens, Greece, Socrates's life is chronicled through only a few sources—the dialogues of Plato and Xenophon and the plays of Aristophanes. Socrates was the son of Sophroniscus, an Athenian stone mason and sculptor, and Phaenarete, a midwife. Because he wasn't from a noble family, he probably received a basic Greek education and learned his father's craft at a young age.

It is believed Socrates worked as a mason for many years before he devoted his life to philosophy. Socrates married Xanthippe, a younger woman, who bore him three sons—Lamprocles, Sophroniscus and Menexenus. He writes she was not happy with Socrates's second profession and complained that he wasn't supporting family as a philosopher. By his own words, Socrates had little to do with his sons' upbringing and expressed far more interest in the intellectual development of Athens' young boys.

Athenian law required all able bodied males serve as citizen soldiers, on call for duty from ages 18 until 60. According to Plato, Socrates served in the armored infantry—known as the hoplite—with shield, long spear and face mask. He participated in three military campaigns during the Peloponnesian War, at Delium, Amphipolis, and Potidaea, where he saved the life of Alcibiades, a popular Athenian general. Socrates was known for his courage in battle and fearlessness, a trait that stayed with him throughout his life.

Philosophy

Socrates believed that philosophy should achieve practical results for the greater well-being of society. He attempted to establish an ethical system based on human reason rather than theological doctrine. He pointed out that human choice was motivated by the desire for happiness. Ultimate wisdom comes from knowing oneself. The more a person knows, the greater his or her ability to reason and make choices that will bring true happiness. Socrates believed that this translated into politics with the best form of government being neither a tyranny nor a democracy. Instead, government worked best when ruled by individuals who had the greatest ability, knowledge, and virtue and possessed a complete understanding of themselves.

For Socrates, Athens was a classroom and he went about asking questions of the elite and common man alike, seeking to arrive at political and ethical truths. Socrates didn't lecture about what he knew. In fact, he claimed to be ignorant because he had no ideas, but wise because he recognized his own ignorance. He asked questions of his fellow Athenians in a dialectic method (the Socratic Method) which compelled the audience to think through a problem to a logical conclusion. Sometimes the answer seemed so obvious, it made Socrates's opponents look foolish. For this, he was admired by some and vilified by others.

During Socrates's life, Athens was going through a dramatic transition from hegemony in the classical world to its decline after a humiliating defeat by Sparta in the Peloponnesian War. Athenians entered a period of instability and doubt about their identity and place in the world. As a result, they clung to past glories, notions of wealth, and a fixation with physical beauty. Socrates attacked these values with his insistent emphasis on the greater importance of the mind. While many Athenians admired Socrates's challenges to Greek conventional wisdom and the humorous way he went about it, an equal number grew angry and felt he threatened their way of life and uncertain future.

Execution

The jury was not swayed by Socrates's defense and convicted him by a vote of 280 to 221. Possibly the defiant tone of his defense contributed to the verdict and he made things worse during the deliberation over his punishment. Athenian law allowed a convicted citizen to propose an alternative punishment to the one called for by the prosecution and the jury would decide. Instead of proposing he be exiled, Socrates suggested he be honored by the city for his contribution to their enlightenment and be paid for his services. The jury was not amused and sentenced him to death by drinking a mixture of poison hemlock.

Before Socrates's execution, friends offered to bribe the guards and rescue him so he could flee into exile. He declined, stating he wasn't afraid of death, felt he would be no better off if in exile and said he was still a loyal citizen of Athens, willing to abide by its laws, even the ones that condemned him to death. Plato described Socrates's execution in his Phaedo dialogue: Socrates drank the hemlock mixture without hesitation. Numbness slowly crept into his body until it reached his heart. Shortly before his final breath, Socrates described his death as a release of the soul from the body.

❑

Contents

The Land of Tumultuous Life

The earliest stages of settlement and social evolution occurred in Greece (Ellada, Hellas) between 10,000 and 3,000 B.C., building the foundation for major advances that were to begin shortly thereafter. People from the Near East, primarily Anatolia, settled in Greece. Groups from Central Europe also moved into the area. Larger villages that were built between 3,500 and 3,000 B.C., show that in that period society was becoming more complex, and that an elite group was forming. Shortly thereafter, craft specialists began to appear, and the form of social organization shifted from tribalism to chiefdoms. Population increased in this period at a slow rate.

The second millennium B.C. saw the evolution of two powerful Greek civilizations, the Minoan in Crete Island and the Mycenaean on the mainland. During the early Bronze Age (3,000-2,200 B.C.), major changes occurred in both Crete and mainland Greece. In both cases, there is evidence of rapid population growth associated with the establishment of trade connections across the Aegean Sea to Anatolia and the Near East. The Cyclades (Kuklat deV, Kiklades)—islands between Crete and the mainland, were settled at this time and seem to have flourished as stepping stones between Europe and Asia. Both the Cyclades and the mainland developed complex societies with skilled craftsmen and political elites.

The civilization that developed in Crete is called Minoan after the mythical King Minos (Mi.nwV). About 2,000 B.C. the Minoans began constructing the palaces that became their trademark. The palace-building period lasted until about 1,450 B.C., included flourishing economic, political, and social organization and active trade in the eastern Mediterranean, as well as the first appearance of writing in the Greek world. In the latter part of this period, Minoan traders ventured as far west as Spain. The large, ornate palaces had a distinctive design, were

built at population centers and were the scene of elaborate religious ceremonies. The destruction of many of the society's palaces by a severe earthquake began the period of decay. The rival Mycenaean civilization took control of Crete's Mediterranean commerce, and by 1,200 B.C. development of the Minoan culture ceased.

Developments in the eighth century B.C. enabled states to re-emerge. The ports of Argos and Corinth, on the eastern shore of the Peloponnesus, grew very fast. Trade with the Near East began to flourish, and increased domestic production enabled new, wealthy elite to rise. Commercial activity centred on the acquisition of metals from the Near East for the manufacture of luxury goods. In this process, the Greeks came in contact with and adopted the alphabet of the Phoenicians, as well as other innovations that accelerated change in Greek civilization.

The civilization that took root on the mainland is called Mycenaean (Mnkh ~ nai Kerkira). The Mycenaeans, an Indo-European group, were the first speakers of the Greek language. The Mycenaean society was at its zenith in the thirteenth and fourteenth centuries B.C. Mycenaeans stressed military excellence and conquered Knossos and the rest of Crete.

The top-heavy system, whose elite based their power solely on military might, contained the seeds of its own destruction.

Between 1,250 and 1,150 B.C., a combination of peasant rebellions and internal warfare destroyed all the Mycenaean palace citadels. Some were reoccupied, but on a much smaller scale; others disappeared forever. The precise circumstances of these events are unknown, but historians speculate that the top-heavy system, whose elite based their power solely on military might, contained the seeds of its destruction.

In the Dark Age that followed most people lived in small communities in remote areas, supported by subsistence farming. Organizationally, Greece was a chiefdom society. Most trade and contacts with cultures in the Near East and elsewhere lapsed.

Between 750 and 500 B.C., the Greeks founded colonies in many parts of the Mediterranean Basin and the Black Sea, and started to exert their cultural influence, which remains in these regions to the present day. Around 730 B.C., permanent Greek colonies were established, based on the metals trade at Ischia and Pithecusai on the coast of Italy. Shortly thereafter, Corinth sent out agricultural settlers to Corfu (Ketrknra, Kerkira) off the coast of northwest Greece and to Syracuse in Sicily. These settlements set the trend for the earliest colonization movement to the west. Southern Italy and Sicily became known as Magna Graecia (Metgatlh 'EllatV Great Greece) because of the extent and density of colonization that followed the initial ventures.

More than 150 colonies were established in Italy, along the coast of northern Greece, in the Bosporus, and on the Black Sea coast. The chief incentive for colonization was the need for additional land for agriculture and living space to accommodate population growth. Colonies established by other civilizations, such as Miletus in Asia Minor, also challenged the Greeks to expand.

The concept of the polis (potltV, city-state) began to evolve with the development of aristocratic clans to replace chiefdoms. Clan rivalries yielded single powerful figures that were termed tyrants because they achieved domination in outright power struggles within the aristocratic group and among clan centres. Because they often were marginal clan members, the success of the tyrants created a new criterion for power—ability rather than birth. This change was a crucial element in the development of the polis, which came to be a politically unified community covering an average of 200 square kilometres and based on a small urban centre. When the tyrants were overthrown after one to three generations, the institutionalized structure they created remained and became an important legacy to the modern world.

Sparta and Athens built states that included wider sectors of society in their political activity and the basis of democracy was laid.

Mythical King Minos

In the eighth century and early seventh century B.C., Sparta began to develop as a militant polis, with a rigid social structure and a government that included an assembly representing all citizens. Meanwhile, Athens became the largest polis, combining several regions of the peninsula of Attica. Under the leadership of the aristocrat Solon (Sotlwn), Athens developed a social system in which power was based on wealth rather than aristocratic birth. Citizens of various wealth categories were allotted different positions of power. Thus, in different ways, Sparta and Athens built states that included wider sectors of society in their political activity than had any previous society, and the basis of democracy was laid.

The consolidation of the Persian Empire under Kurosh-e Bozorg (Cyrus the Great) in the sixth century B.C. posed a major threat to the fledgling states of Greece. The resolution of the clash between East and West was to shape the entire future of the region. For the Greeks, it was a question of survival; for the Persians, on the other hand, occupation of Greece was simply part of their imperial plan. Nonetheless, the Persian Wars are significant because they resulted in a separation between Greece and the Near East after centuries of fruitful interaction.

The First Persian War in 490 B.C. was a brief affair. Persia sent a small force, about 20,000 infantry and 800 cavalry to punish Athens for its participation in a raid in Asia Minor. The Greeks met this force with 10,000 troops at the plain of Marathon (Maraqw~noV) on the west coast of the Attic Peninsula. The combination of Greek tactics, the superiority of their armor, and the new phalanx formation, proved decisive in the battle; and the Persians were routed.

Pheidippides (Feidippi.dhV), Athenian messenger, was sent to Sparta to request help when the Persians landed at Marathon. He ran 240 km (150 miles) in two days. He then ran the 40 km (26 miles) from the battlefield, near the town of Marathon, to Athens, to announce the Greek victory over Persia in the Battle of Marathon, with the message "we have won" (Nenikhtkamen, Nenikékamen). He died of exhaustion on the spot after conveying the message.

The Second Persian War of 481-479 B.C. was a very different proposition. Khashayar Shah (XetrxhV, Xerxes), the king of Persia, invaded Greece with a huge fleet and an army of over 100,000 men. After overcoming fierce Spartan resistance at Thermopylae, the Persians occupied central Greece and the Greeks retreated south to the Peloponnesus. The Attic Peninsula was taken and Athens sacked. On the seas, however, the Greeks completely destroyed the Persian fleet in the Bay of Salamis. Khashayar Shah retreated hastily to Asia then suffered a great land defeat the next year at the Battle of Plataia, in which the superiority of Greek armour and tactics was the deciding factor. Persian expansionism never threatened Greece again.

The Persian Wars ruptured a vibrant cultural zone and the concept of a divided Asia and Europe became permanent.

The most important result of the Persian Wars was a barrier between Greece and the Near East that ruptured a vibrant cultural zone including Phoenicia, Lydia, Egypt, and other cultures of the Near East. The barrier would not be broken until the middle of the next century, and the concept of a divided Asia and Europe became permanent.

Once the Persian menace had been removed, petty squabbling began amongst the members of the Hellenic League. Sparta, feeling that its job was completed, left the association, and Athens assumed domination of the league. Under the leadership of Themistocles and Kimon, Athens reformed the alliance into a new body called the Delian League, an association of approximately 150 city-states, under the leadership of Athens. By using monetary contributions from other member states to build its own military forces, Athens essentially transformed the Hellenic League into its own empire.

❑

The Travelling Teachers

The political and social upheaval caused by the Persian Wars as well as continued strife between Athens and Sparta had at least one unintended consequence. In the 5th century B.C., a flood of new ideas poured into Athens. In general, these new ideas came as a result of an influx of Ionian thinkers into the Attic peninsula. Athens had become the intellectual and artistic center of the Greek world. Furthermore, by the mid-5th century B.C., it had become more common for advanced thinkers to reject traditional explanations of the world of nature.

As a result of the experience of a century of war, religious beliefs declined. Gods and goddesses were no longer held in the same regard as they had been a century earlier. The Persian and Peloponnesian Wars taught that the actions of men and women determine their own destiny, and not Moira (moi ~ ra, fate). Meanwhile, more traditional notions of right and wrong were called into question, and all of this was expressed in Hellenic tragedy and comedy.

Everything in the universe was made of water and resolves itself into water. The gods are omitted from the origins of nature.

The pre-Socratic philosophers came from the city of Miletus (Mi.lhtoV) in the region of Ionia (Iwni.a, region of central coastal Anatolia in present-day Turkey). Miletus was a prominent trading depot and its people had direct contact with the ideas of the Near East. Around 600 B.C., Milesian thinkers "discovered" speculation after asking a simple but profound question: "What exists?"

It was the Ionian natural philosopher, Thales of Miletus (624-548), who answered that everything in the universe was made of water and resolves itself into water. What was so revolutionary about Thales was that he omitted the gods from his account of the origins of nature. It is also necessary to point out that Thales committed none of his views to writing.

Anaximander of Miletus (611-547 B.C.) rejected Thales, and argued instead that an indefinite substance—the boundless—was the source of all things. According to Anaximander, the cold and wet condensed to form the earth while the hot and dry formed the moon, sun and stars. The heat from the fire in the skies dried the earth and shrank the seas. It is a rather fantastic scheme; but at least Anaximander sought natural explanations for the origin of the natural world.

Both Thales and Anaximander were "matter" philosophers—they believed that everything had its origin in a material substance. Pythagoras of Samos (580-507 B.C.) did not find that nature of things in material substances but in mathematical relationships. The Pythagoreans, who lived in Greek cities in southern Italy, discovered that the intervals in the musical scale could be expressed mathematically and that this principle could be extended to the universe. In other words, the universe contained an inherent mathematical order. What we witness in the Pythagoreans is the emphasis on form rather than matter, and here we move from sense perception to the logic of mathematics.

Parmenides of Elea (515-450 B.C.) also challenged the fundamental views of the Ionian philosophers that all things emerged from one substance. What Parmenides did was to apply logic to the arguments of the Pythagoreans, thus setting the groundwork of formal logic. He argued that reality is one, eternal and unchanging. We "know" reality not by the senses, which are capable of deception, but through the human mind, not through experience, but through reason. As we shall see, this concept shall become central to the philosophic thought of Plato.

We "know" reality not by the senses, which are capable of deception, but through the human mind, not through experience, but through reason.

Perhaps the most important of all the Pre-Socratic philosophers was Heraclitus of Ephesus (500 B.C.). Known as "the weeping philosopher" because of his pessimistic view of human nature and "the dark one" because of the mystical obscurity of his thought, Heraclitus wrote On Nature, fragments of which we still possess. Whereas the Pythagoreans had emphasized harmony, Heraclitus suggested that life was maintained by a tension of opposites, fighting a continuous battle in which neither side could win a final victory. Movement and the flux of change were unceasing for individuals, but the structure of the cosmos constant. This law of individual flux within a permanent universal framework was guaranteed by the Logos, an intelligent governing principle materially embodied as fire, and identified with soul or life.

Fire is the primordial element out of which all else has arisen—change (becoming) is the first principle of the universe. Cratylus, a follower of Heraclitus, once made the remark that "You cannot step twice into the same river." The water will be different water the second time, and if we call the river the same, it is because we see its reality in its form. The logical conclusion of this is the opposite of flux, that is, a belief in an absolute, unchanging reality of which the world of change and movement is only a quasi-existing phantom, phenomenal, not real.

Persian Emperor Kurosh-e Bozorg

Democritus of Abdera (460-370 B.C.) "the laughing philosopher" argued that knowledge was derived through sense perception—the senses illustrate to us that change does occur in nature. However, Democritus also retained Parmenides' confidence in human reason. His universe consisted of empty space and an infinite number of atoms (a-temnw, a-tomos—the uncuttable). Eternal and indivisible, these atoms moved in the void of space. An atomic theory to the core, Democritus saw all matter constructed of atoms which accounted for all change in the natural world.

What the Pre-Socratic thinkers from Thales to Democritus had done was nothing less than amazing—they had given to nature a rational and non-mythical foundation. This new approach allowed a critical analysis of theories, whereas mythical explanations relied on blind faith alone. Such a spirit even found its way into medicine, where the Greek physician Hippocrates of Cos (460-377 B.C.) was able to distinguish between magic and medicine. Physicians observed ill patients, classified symptoms and then made predictions about the course of a disease. For instance, of epilepsy, he wrote: "It is not, in my opinion, any more divine or more sacred than other diseases, but has a natural cause, and its supposed divine origin is due to men's inexperience, and to their wonder at its peculiar character."

The Golden Age of Athens, the age of Pericles (Periklh ~ V, meaning surrounded by glory), which lasted from 445 to 431 B.C. has come to symbolize perfection in human civilized life. By this time, Athens had become a democracy as the culmination of a large struggle between a small number of land owning families of the aristocracy and great numbers of the poor. Pericles, elected annually as the first citizen of the state, skilfully maintained political rights for all citizens, for the aristocracy and for commoners, for rich and for poor, although not for women or slaves. Pericles promoted the arts and literature; this was a chief reason Athens holds the reputation of being the educational and cultural centre of the ancient Greek world. He started an ambitious project that built most of the surviving structures on the Acropolis, including the Parthenon. This project beautified the city, exhibited its glory, and gave work to the people. The poor were held to be virtuous and as capable as the rich. Of the poor, the Greek dramatist Aeschylus (Ai.scutloV) wrote in one of his famous plays: "Justice shines in houses grimy with smoke." And the philosopher Protagoras (PrwtagotraV) said: "Anyone who is just and reverent is qualified to give advice on public affairs."

Pericles's moderate policy in time ran into opposition with extremists on both the aristocratic right and the democratic left. But a strong sense of loyalty to Athens unified the city politically when war with Sparta broke out in the spring of 431 B.C. At this time most of the communities of Greece were under the leadership of either the Athenian Empire, which was democratic, commercial, and industrial, or the Spartan Empire, which was authoritarian, militaristic, and agricultural. The Peloponnesian War as it developed became clearly a struggle between Athenian democracy and the authoritarianism of Sparta, which was ruled by the military elite with absolute power. In the second year of the war, an uncontrollable plague broke out in Athens which was overcrowded and rapidly becoming impoverished. Democratic Athens finally surrendered to Sparta in 404 B.C. Instead of ruining Athens, Sparta installed as the conquered city's rulers a collaborationist regime of anti-democratic Athenian aristocrats, who became known as the Thirty Tyrants (30 tutrannoi). These men came from the class of aristocrats that had traditionally despised democracy and admired oligarchy.

Into such an atmosphere of change came the travelling teachers, the Sophists. The Sophists were a diverse bunch - some hailed from the Athenian polis or other city-states, but the majority came from Ionia, in Asia Minor. The Sophists were men whose responsibility it was to train and educate the sons of Athenian citizens. There were no formal schools as we know them today. Instead, these were peripatetic schools, meaning that the instructor would walk with students and talk with them - for a fee, of course. The Sophists taught the skills (Sojía, sophia) of rhetoric and oratory. Both of these arts were essential for the education of the Athenian citizenry. After all, it was the sons of the citizens who would eventually find themselves debating important issues in the Assembly and the Council of Five Hundred. Rhetoric can be described as the art of composition, while oratory was the art of public speaking.

The Sophists taught the subtle art of persuasion. They would argue eloquently - and prove a position whether that position was correct or incorrect. What mattered was persuasion and not truth. The Sophists were also relativists. They believed that there was no such thing as a universal or absolute truth, valid at all times. According to Protagoras (485-411 B.C.), "Man is the measure of all things." Everything is relative and there are no values because man, individual man, is the measure of all things. Nothing is good or bad since everything depends on the individual. Gorgias of Leontini (485-380 B.C.), was a well-paid teacher of rhetoric and famous for his saying that a man could not know anything. And if he could, he could not describe it, and if he could describe it, no one would understand him.

At their very best, the Sophists challenged the accepted values of the fifth century B.C. They wanted the freedom to sweep away old conventions as a way to having a better understanding of the universe, the gods and man. The Sophists have been compared with the philosophers of the 18th century Enlightenment who also used criticism and reason to wipe out anything they deemed was contrary to human reason. Regardless of what we think of the Sophists as a group or individually, they certainly did have the cumulative effect of further degrading a mythical understanding of the universe and of man.

❑

The Pursuit of Truth

From the ranks of the Sophists came Socrates, perhaps the most noble and wisest Athenian to have ever lived. His father was Sophroniscus (Swjroni.skoV), a stone cutter, and his mother, Phaenarete (Fainareth), was a midwife. Sophroniscus was a close friend of the son of Aristides the Just (550-468 B.C.), and the young Socrates was familiar with members of the circle of Pericles. In his youth he fought as a hoplite at Potidaea (432-429 B.C.), Delium (424 B.C.) and Amphipolis (422 B.C.) during the Peloponnesian Wars.

Socrates' later absorption in philosophy made him neglect his private affairs and he eventually fell to a level of comparative poverty. He was perhaps more in love with the study of philosophy than with his family. His wife Xanthippe (Xanqi.pph) was much younger than Socrates, perhaps by as much as forty years. She was quarrelsome, nagging and ill-tempered. Socrates was, however, concerned with the future of his three sons.

Socrates was remarkable for living the life he preached. Taking no fees, Socrates would start and dominate an argument for the sake of imparting wisdom. He did this wherever and

Ruins at Rhodes

whenever the young and intelligent would listen. He was so renowned for his wisdom that people asked his advice on matters of practical conduct and educational problems.

Socrates was remarkable for living the life he preached.

Socrates was not an attractive man—he was snub-nosed, prematurely bald, and overweight. But, he was strong in body, and the intellectual master of every one with whom he came into contact. The Athenian youth flocked to his side as he walked the paths of the Agora (Greek term for place of assembly). They clung to his every word and gesture.

In 399 B.C., Socrates was charged with impiety by a jury of five hundred of his fellow citizens. His most famous student, Plato (Plattwn), tells us, that he was charged "as an evil-doer and curious person, searching into things under the earth and above the heavens; and making the worse appear the better cause, and teaching all this to others." He was convicted to death by a margin of six votes. Oddly enough, the jury offered Socrates the chance to pay a small fine for his impiety. He rejected it. He also rejected the pleas of Plato and other students who had a boat waiting for him at Piraeus (PeiraiatV) harbour that would take him to freedom. But Socrates refused to break the law. What kind of citizen would he be if he refused to accept the judgment of the jury? No citizen at all. He spent his last days with his friends before he drank the fatal dose of hemlock.

The charge made against Socrates—disbelief in the state's gods—implied un-Athenian activities which would corrupt the young and the state if preached publicly. Meletus, the citizen who brought the indictment, sought precedents in the impiety trials of Pericles' friends. Although Socrates was neither a heretic, unconventional or unorthodox, nor an agnostic or disbeliever, there was prejudice against him. He also managed to provoke hostility. For instance, the Delphic oracle is said to have told Chaerephon, a loyal friend and follower of Socrates, that no man was wiser than Socrates. During his trial Socrates had the audacity to use this as justification of his examination of the conduct of all Athenians, claiming that in exposing their falsehoods, he had proved the god right - he, atleast, knew that he knew nothing. Although this episode smacks of Socrates' well-known irony, he clearly did believe that his mission was divinely inspired.

Socrates has been described as a gadfly (muopa, a term for people who upset the status quo by posing upsetting or novel questions or just being an irritant). The reason why this charge is somewhat justified is that he challenged his students to think for themselves—to use their minds to answer questions. He did not reveal answers. He did not reveal truth. "Many of his questions were, on the surface, quite simple: What is courage? What is virtue? What is duty? But what Socrates discovered, and what he taught his students to discover, was that most people could not answer these fundamental questions to his satisfaction, yet all of them claimed to be courageous, virtuous and dutiful. It should be one of the functions of a teacher to open vistas before his pupils, showing them the possibility of activities that will be as delightful as they are useful," wrote Bertrand Russell about Socrates.

Socrates wrote nothing himself. What we know of him comes from the writings of two of his closest friends, Xenophon (Xenojw ~ n) and Plato. Although Xenophon (430-354 B.C.) did write four short portraits of Socrates, it is almost due to Plato alone that we know anything of Socrates. Plato (427-347 B.C.) was perhaps Socrates' most famous student. He was twenty-eight years old when Socrates was put to death. At the age of forty, Plato established a school at Athens for the education of Athenian youth. The Academy, as it was called, remained in existence from 387 B.C. to A.D. 529, when it was closed by Justinian, the Byzantine emperor.

Our knowledge of Socrates comes to us from numerous dialogues which Plato wrote after 399 B.C. In nearly every dialogue - and there are more than thirty that we know about - Socrates is the main speaker. The style of the Plato's dialogue is important – it is the Socratic style that he employs throughout. A Socratic dialogue takes the form of question-answer. It is a dialectical style as well. Socrates would argue both sides of a question in order to arrive at a conclusion. Then that conclusion is argued against another assumption and so on.

Knowledge is present in the human mind at birth. It is not so much that we "learn" things in our daily experience, but that we "recollect" them.

There is a reason why Socrates employed this style, as well as why Plato recorded his experience with Socrates in the form of a dialogue. Socrates taught Plato a great many things, but one of the things Plato more or less discovered on his own was that mankind is born with knowledge. That is, knowledge is present in the human mind at birth. It is not so much that we "learn" things in our daily experience, but that we "recollect" them. In other words, this knowledge is already there. This may explain why Socrates did not give his students answers, but only questions. His job was not to teach truth but to show his students how they could "pull" truth out of their own minds. It is for this reason that Socrates often considered himself a midwife in the labour of knowledge. And this is the point of the dialogues. For only in conversation, only in dialogue, can truth and wisdom come to the surface.

Socrates insisted many times that he was not an authority regarding anything. Almost without exception, he held that he was simply trying to understand the essence of whatever issue or question was at that time being discussed. When a seemingly wise man would make a bold proclamation regarding love, virtue, justice, or some other philosophical consideration, Socrates would respond by asking a simple question. When Meno (Menwn), in the dialogue that bears his name, asks Socrates, "Can virtue be taught?" Socrates asks, "Can you tell me what virtue is?" When Meno replies with a list of answers, Socrates notes that Meno has made something that was one into something that was many—not very illustrative. He asks Meno if there is a single, unified definition of virtue. Thus begins a friendly dialogue (not merely a technique), that discusses not only the essence of virtue in men, but also examines the very nature of knowledge and learning itself.

"Can virtue be taught?"

"Can you tell me what virtue is?"

Thus, the Socratic Method is a conversation, a discussion, wherein two or more people assist one another in finding the answers to difficult questions. Why did Socrates proceed in this manner? Despite his many claims of ignorance Socrates understood better than those with whom he spoke that it was not enough simply to "learn" facts, to memorize lessons, or to parrot lectures. To know truly, to seek wisdom, one must work toward

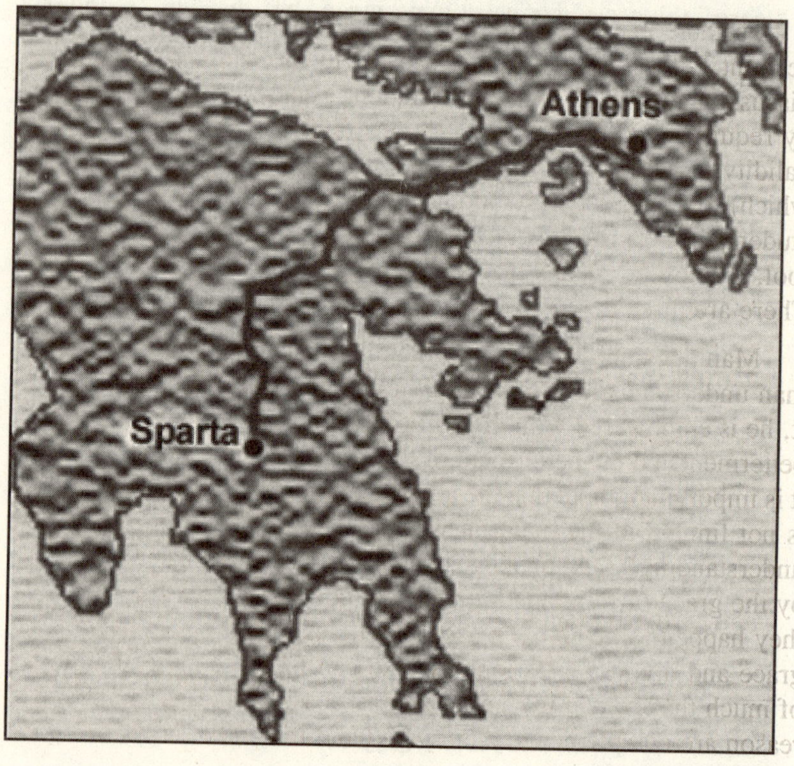

understanding. The question "what" can lead us to see what we do and what we do not know. The question "why" can lead us to understand our world in a more full and fundamental manner.

If a student tells you that the square on the hypotenuse of a right-angled triangle is equal to the squares on the two remaining sides taken together, he would, or course, be correct. But if you ask this student "why" this is so, would he be able to give you that answer? If he cannot, then he has memorized an "answer" that, while possessing certain utility, does not of itself provide understanding of causes. But if he gives any one of a number of reasoned explanations why the right triangle has the property described, then he demonstrates not only his understanding of causes, but also the ability to communicate that understanding to others.

Further, his understanding is greater to the degree that his account is the one that comes closest to the cause itself. The discussion method facilitates the student's quest for understanding by requiring him to answer questions on his own, to ponder the validity of what others have said or written, and (not the least of which) to give reasoned support of his own opinion to the other students in the group. While the discussion method is a powerful tool, it is by no means the only activity by which people learn. There are three distinct activities by which learning takes place.

Man does not forget that which he understands; and when a man understands both the world he lives in and his true place in it, he is empowered with the ability to choose rightly for his own betterment and the betterment of those around him. Additionally, it is important to note that the activity of increasing understanding is not limited to the material world. The phrase "faith seeking understanding" acknowledges that even those things we know by the grace of religious faith are not contrary to reason, even if they happen to be above reason. Articles of faith are known by grace and divine revelation, yet one can increase understanding of much that is held by faith. This is possible because faith and reason are complementary; they go hand in hand.

It is a fact of human nature that a man often thinks he knows something until he is forced to articulate it. In other words, an indistinct "knowledge" of something — which is really little more than a feeling — reveals its true nature in the process of being brought into the light of discussion. The beauty of the process is that in finding the limit of our knowledge we not only discover where our ignorance ends, but also where our true knowledge begins.

❑

What is Piety?

Euthyphro is one of Plato's early dialogues, dated around 399 B.C. It features Socrates and Euthyphro, a man known for being a religious expert. The dialogue is set near the king-archon's court, where the two men encounter each other. They are both there for preliminary hearings before possible trials. Euthyphro has come to lay murder charges against his father, as his father had allowed one of his workers to die without proper care and attention. The worker had killed a slave belonging to the family estate on the island of Naxos, and while Euthyphro's father waited to hear from the authorities on his course of action, the man died bound and gagged in a ditch.

Socrates expresses his astonishment at the confidence of a man able to take his own father to court on such a serious charge. In what may be perceived as a tongue-in-cheek fashion, Socrates states that Euthyphro obviously has a clear understanding of what is pious (tò ò'sion, to osion) and impious (atno tsion, to anosion). Since Socrates himself is facing a charge of impiety, by worshipping gods not approved by the state, and is unclear on what holiness is, he hopes to learn from Euthyphro. Socrates invites Euthyphro to put forward definitions of holiness which the two can then discuss.

Euthyphro offers as his first definition of piety what he is doing now, that is, prosecuting his father for manslaughter. Socrates rejects this because it is not a definition; it is only an example or instance of piety. It does not provide the fundamental characteristic which makes pious things pious.

Euthyphro then gives a second definition: Piety is what the gods approve of. Socrates applauds this definition because it is expressed in a general form, but criticizes it on the grounds that the gods disagree among themselves as to what meets their approval. This would mean that a particular action, disputed by the gods, would be both pious and impious at the same time — a logically impossible situation.

Euthyphro tries to argue against Socrates' criticism by pointing out that not even the gods would disagree amongst themselves that someone who kills without justification should be punished, but Socrates argues that disputes would still arise — over just how much justification there actually was, and hence the same action could still be both pious and impious.

"Is the pious loved by the gods because it is pious? Or is it pious because it is loved by the gods?"

Euthyphro overcomes Socrates' objection by slightly amending his second definition. Thus the third definition reads: What all the gods approve of is pious, and what they all disapprove of is impious. At this point Socrates introduces the "Euthyphro dilemma" by asking the crucial question: "Is the pious loved by the gods because it is pious? Or is it pious because it is loved by the gods?" He uses a typical Socratic technique, analogy or comparison, to make his question clearer and gets Euthyphro to agree that we call a carried thing carried simply because it is carried, not because it possesses some inherent characteristic or property that we could call "carried". What he is trying to get Euthyphro to see is that we carry something that is already there.

Battle of Marathon

This thing exists without our carrying it; our carrying does not bring it into existence. So as far as piety is concerned, we approve or disapprove of something which is already, in some sense, there; our approving, by itself, does not make an action pious. The approval follows from our recognition that an action is pious, not the other way around. Or, to put it more simply, the piety comes before the approval, yet in Euthyphro's definition it comes after the approval and is a result of the approval. Euthyphro's definition is, therefore, flawed.

Without realizing that it contradicts his third definition, Euthyphro at this point agrees that the gods approve an action because it is pious. Socrates argues that the unanimous approval of the gods is merely an attribute of piety; it is not part of its defining characteristics. It does not define the essence of piety, what piety actually is. Thus, it does not give the idea of piety.

In the second half of the discussion Socrates himself suggests a definition of piety, namely that piety is a part of justice: Piety belongs to those actions we call just or morally good. However, there are more than simply pious actions that we call just or morally good; for example, bravery, and concern for others and so on. What is it, asks Socrates that makes piety different from all those other actions that we call just?

Euthyphro then suggests that piety is concerned with looking after the gods, but Socrates immediately raises the objection that "looking after", if used in its ordinary sense, which Euthyphro agrees that it is, would imply that when you perform an act of piety you make one of the gods better — a dangerous example of hubris, which gods frowned upon. Euthyphro claims that caring for involves service. When questioned by Socrates as to exactly what is the end product of piety, Euthyphro can only fall back on his earlier claim: Piety is what finds approval amongst all the gods.

Euthyphro then proposes another definition: Piety, he says, is a sort of sacrifice and prayer. He puts forward the notion of piety as a form of commerce: Giving the gods gifts and asking favours of them in turn. Socrates presses Euthyphro to state what benefit the gods get from the gifts humans give to them. Euthyphro replies that they are not that sort of gift at all, but rather "honour, esteem and gratitude". In other words, as he admits, piety is intimately bound up with what the gods approve of. The discussion has come full circle; Euthyphro rushes off to another engagement, and Socrates faces a charge of impiety.

What makes of the Euthyphro a philosophical work is precisely that it is not anything of what most people expect of a philosophical work. It does not advance a thesis; it does not draw inferences from a proposition or a set of propositions; it does not establish a theory or present arguments in support of a hypothesis.

A philosophical work does not aim to arrive at conclusions, but to help us gaze within ourselves with clearer eyes.

A philosophical work, true to Socratic dialectic, does not seek to arrive at a definite conclusion, or to prove or uphold a thesis or a set of theses, but to subject one's own and others' beliefs, presuppositions, and accepted notions to searching examination, to illumine obscure nooks and crannies in one's own mind and others' minds. The end is not to arrive at conclusions, but to help us gaze within ourselves with clearer eyes.

A modern reader will readily understand that dialectic means a co-operative inquiry carried on in conversation between two or more minds that are equally bent, not on getting the better of the argument, but on arriving at the truth. A tentative suggestion, hypothesis, put forward by one speaker is corrected and improved until the full meaning is clearly stated. The criticism that follows may end in complete rejection or lead on to another suggestion which, if the examination has been skillfully conducted, ought to approach nearer to the truth.

This is a good description of the procedure of dialectical discourse, which is basically true of all genuine philosophical discourse however conducted. But the phrases 'arriving at the truth' and 'to approach nearer to the truth' are problematic. There is no objective truth to be arrived at. The end of proper philosophical discourse is to achieve a fuller awareness of our presuppositions, a clearer understanding of the fundamental notions and principles on which we base our judgments. Those fundamental notions and principles cannot be discovered in anything external to the mind and are not amenable to proof. To argue with a view to establishing their truth or revealing their falsity is vain. They rest in their own self-evidence. The question to be raised with regard to them is not a question of truth or

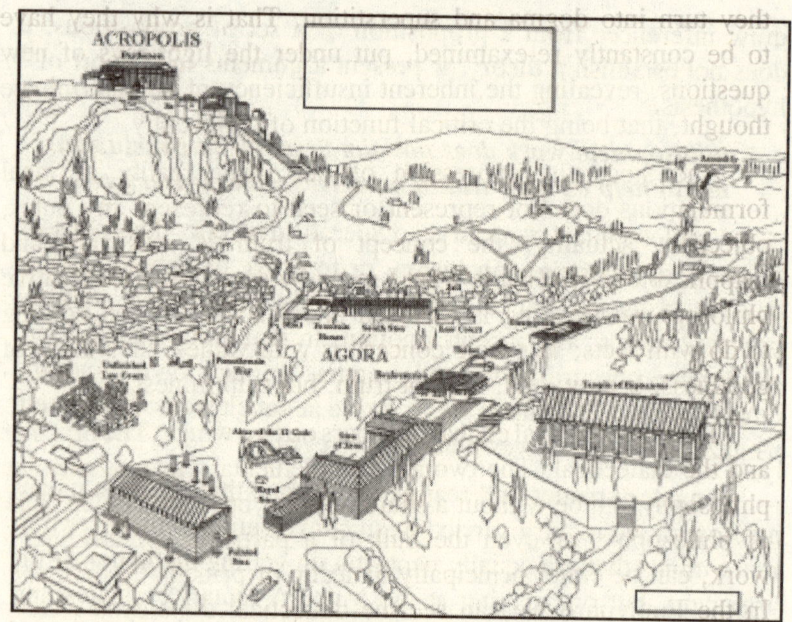

Athens in the times of Socrates

falsity, but one of value and sufficiency and viability. The critical question to be posed in assessing a philosophical view should be: What kind of world does that view give us to live in? What kind of life does it offer? What level of intelligibility does it secure for us?

Does this mean that philosophical thought has no positive content whatever? No. It can rest in no definitive formulation whatever. The searching examination is the whole of the philosophical act: That perpetuated act is a constant affirmation and realization of the reality of human intelligence and the integrity of the human mind. That is our whole reality and the ground of our proper worth. That reality finds creative expression in ideals and principles and theoretical models, rooted in our reality and 'true' in so far as they are expressions of that reality. But their particular formulations are necessarily always relative and contingent. Taken as final and absolute, as 'true', they turn into dogma and superstition. That is why they have to be constantly re-examined, put under the light-rays of new questions, revealing the inherent insufficiency of all determinate thought, that being the critical function of philosophy.

And since the expression of our inner reality in ideal formulations does not represent or seek to represent any outer, objective, actuality, the concept of truth is irrelevant and inapplicable to it. That is what I mean by saying that all creative philosophical thinking is mythical and oracular. It has nothing to do with facts; its whole concern is with values, the values of goodness, beauty, and, no! not truth, but truthfulness.

The philosophical endeavour soars on two wings: The oracular and the dialectical. The two are complementary and no genuine philosophy can be without a share of both, but a particular work of philosophy, or even the bulk of a particular philosopher's work, can be either principally dialectic or principally oracular. In the Euthyphro we can see the dialectical dimension clearly illustrated, but we can also glimpse the oracular dimension, not only in the ideal of God or the gods as necessarily good but also and markedly in the principle that moral values must be autonomous. This was the insight that later formed the core of moral philosophy.

Ignorance is not lack of knowledge; it is disknowledge instilled into the soul by bad upbringing and bad education, consisting in false values and notions. and beliefs.

Socrates' life-mission was to combat Amathia, ignorance, by helping his interlocutors examine themselves. Amathia, the evil is not lack of knowledge; it is disknowledge instilled into the soul by bad upbringing and bad education, consisting in false values and notions and beliefs. But the process is not purely negative. The philosopher introduces, actually creates, concepts, conceptual distinctions, ideal patterns, which expand, enrich, deepen the capacity of the mind to infuse meaning into the givennesses of experience. Such concepts, conceptual distinctions, and ideal patterns, are not derived from the outer world and therefore cannot be in any way verified or proved. Again, they are not 'knowledge' imparted to the learner. If the learner receives them as factual knowledge they turn into dogmatic superstitions, a new Amathia. When the learner sees them as creative developments of her/his own mind, they become forms of intelligibility under which the mind can translate more of the chaos of the givennesses of experience into the cosmos of intelligence.

❑

The Examined Life

Because of his political associations with an earlier regime, the Athenian democracy put Socrates on trial, charging him with undermining state religion and corrupting young people. The speech he offered in his own defence, as reported in Plato's Apologhma apologi.a (Apology), provides us with many reminders of the central features of Socrates' approach to philosophy and its relation to practical life.

At the trial for his life in 399 B.C., Socrates astonished his listeners by appearing, despite his vigorous defence, to deliberately get himself found guilty and condemned to death. What he had said was then a matter of some curiosity, but the Apology is one of those rare works that gracefully bridges the divide between philosophy and literature. The work is less concerned with asserting any particular philosophical doctrines than it is with creating a portrait of the ideal philosopher. On trial, with his life at stake, Socrates maintains his cool and unwaveringly defends his way of life as unassailably just. This speech has served as inspiration and justification for philosophical thinkers ever since.

Socrates usually addresses the jury as Athenian men. The *Apology* begins with Socrates saying he does not know if the men of Athens have been persuaded by his accusers. This first sentence is crucial to the theme of the entire speech. Plato often begins his Socratic dialogues with words which indicate the overall idea of the dialogue. In this case, "I do not know". Indeed, in the *Apology*, Socrates will suggest that philosophy begins with a sincere admission of ignorance, and that whatever wisdom he has, comes from his knowledge that he knows nothing.

Philosophy begins with a sincere admission of ignorance, and that whatever wisdom one has, comes from his knowledge that he knows nothing.

Socrates asks the jury to judge him not by his oratorical skills, but by the truth. Socrates says he will not use ornate words and phrases that are carefully arranged, but will speak the chance thoughts that come into his head. He says he will use the same words that he is heard using at the Agora and the money tables. In spite of his disclaimers, Socrates proves to be a master rhetoric

Athens as viewed from Piraeus

who is not only eloquent and persuasive, but who plays the jury like in charge of an opera. However, the speech, which has won readers to his side for more than two millennia, does not succeed in winning him acquittal. Socrates is famously condemned to death by drinking hemlock, and has been admired for the calm acceptance of his fate.

The three men who brought the charges against Socrates were: Anytus, on behalf of the craftsmen and politicians, Meletus on behalf of the poets, and Lycon on behalf of the rhetoricians.

Socrates says that he has to refute two sets of accusations: The old, longstanding charges that he is a criminal, a busybody, and a curious person who makes inquiries into the earth and sky, and the recent legal charges that he is guilty of corrupting the young, and of believing in supernatural things of his own invention instead of the gods recognized by the State.

Socrates was charged on behalf of the craftsmen and politicians, on behalf of the poets, and on behalf of the rhetoricians.

Socrates says that the old charges stemmed from years of gossip and prejudice against him and hence were unanswerable. These so called 'informal charges' Socrates puts into the style of a formal legal accusation: "Socrates is committing an injustice, in that he inquires into things below the earth and in the sky, and makes the weaker argument the stronger, and teaches others to follow his example". He says that these allegations stem from a certain comic poet, namely Aristophanes. In his play, "The Clouds," Aristophanes lampooned Socrates by presenting him as the paradigm of atheistic, scientific sophistry.

Socrates says that he cannot possibly be mistaken for a sophist because they are wise (or at least thought to be) and highly paid. He says he is poor and claims to know nothing noble and good. The Apology can be divided into three parts. The first part is Socrates' own defense of himself and includes the most famous parts of the text, namely his recounting of the Oracle at Delphi and his cross-examination of Meletus. The second part is the verdict, and the third part is the punishment.

Socrates begins by telling the jurors that their minds were poisoned by his enemies when they were young and impressionable. He says his reputation for sophistry comes from his enemies, all of whom are envious of him, and malicious. He says they must remain nameless, except for Aristophanes, the comic poet. He later answers the charge that he has corrupted the young by arguing that deliberate corruption is an incoherent idea. Socrates says that his problems all began with the oracle. He tells how Chaerephon went to the Oracle at Delphi, to ask if anyone was wiser than Socrates. When Chaerephon reported to Socrates that the god told him there is none wiser, Socrates took this as a riddle. He says that he knew that he had no wisdom "great or small" but that he also knew that it is against the nature of the gods to lie.

Socrates determined that the politicians were impostors, and said that the poets did not understand their own writings.

Socrates then went on a "divine mission" to solve the paradox that an ignorant man could also be the wisest person in town and to clarify the meaning of the Oracles' words, he systematically quizzed the politicians, poets and craftsmen. Socrates determined that the politicians were impostors, and said that the poets did not understand their own writings, like prophets and seers who do not understand what they say. Craftsmen prove to be pretentious too, and Socrates says that he made himself a spokesman for the oracle. He asked himself whether he would rather be an impostor like the people he spoke to, or be himself. Speaking for the oracle, Socrates tells the jury that he would rather be himself than anyone else.

Socrates says that this questioning earned him the reputation of being an annoying busybody. Socrates interpreted his life's mission as proof that true wisdom belongs to the

Socrates

gods and that human wisdom and achievements have little or no value. Having addressed the cause of the prejudice against him, Socrates then tackles the formal charges, corruption of the young and atheism.

Socrates' first move is to accuse his accuser, Meletus (whose name means literally, "the person who cares," or "caring") of not caring about the things he professes to care about. He argues during his interrogation of Meletus that no one would intentionally corrupt another person because they stand to be harmed by him at a later date. The issue of corruption is important for two reasons: First, it appears to be the heart of the charge against him, that he corrupted the young by teaching some version of atheism, and second, Socrates says that if he is convicted, it will be because Aristophanes corrupted the minds of his audience when they were young.

Socrates then proceeds to deal with the second charge, that he is an atheist. He cross-examines Meletus, and extracts a contradiction. He gets Meletus to say that Socrates is an atheist who believes in spiritual agencies and demigods. Socrates announces that he has caught Meletus in a contradiction, and asks the court whether Meletus has designed an intelligence test for him to see if he can identify logical contradictions.

Socrates repeats his claim that it will not be the formal charges which will destroy him, but rather the gossip and slander. He is not afraid of death, because he is more concerned about whether he is acting rightly or wrongly. Further, Socrates argues, those who fear death are showing their ignorance: Death may be a great blessing, but many people fear it as an evil when they cannot possibly know it to be such. Again Socrates points out that his wisdom lies in the fact that he is aware that he does not know.

Socrates states clearly that a lawful superior, whether human or divine, should be obeyed. If there is a clash between the two, however, divine authority should take precedence. "Gentlemen, I am your grateful and devoted servant, but I owe a greater obedience to God than to you; and as long as I draw breath and have my faculties I shall never stop practicing philosophy". Since Socrates has interpreted the Delphic Oracle as singling him out to spur his fellow Athenians to a greater awareness of moral goodness and truth, he will not stop questioning and arguing should the people forbid him to do so, even if they were to withdraw the charges. Nor will he stop questioning his fellow citizens. "Are you not ashamed that you give your attention to acquiring as much money as possible, and similarly with reputation and honour, and give no attention or thought to truth and understanding and the perfection of your soul?"

In a highly inflammatory section of the Apology, Socrates claims that no greater good has happened to Athens than his concern for his fellow citizens, that wealth is a consequence of goodness (and not the other way around), that God does not permit a better man to be harmed by a worse. He goes on to say, in the strongest statement that he gives of his task, that he is a stinging gadfly and the state a lazy horse, "and all day long I will never cease to settle here, there and everywhere, rousing, persuading, and reproving every one of you."

As further evidence of his task, Socrates reminds the court of his daimon (δαι.μων) which he sees as a supernatural experience. He recognises this as partly behind the charge of believing in invented beings. Again Socrates makes no concession to his situation. He would have been well aware that many, if not most, in the courtroom would have viewed this with utmost suspicion.

Socrates claims to never have been a teacher, in the sense of imparting knowledge to others. He cannot therefore be held responsible if any citizen turns bad. If he has corrupted anyone, why have they not come forward to be witnesses? Or if they do not realize that they have been corrupted, why have their relatives not stepped forward on their behalf? Many relatives of the young men associated with him, Socrates points out, are presently in the courtroom to support him.

Socrates concludes this part of the Apology by reminding the jurors that he will not resort to the usual emotive tricks and

Socrates and his Students

arguments. He will not break down in tears, nor will he produce his three sons in the hope of swaying the jurors. He does not fear death; nor will he act in a way contrary to his religious duty. He will rely solely on sound argument and the truth to present his case.

It was the tradition that the prosecution and the defendant each propose a penalty, from which the court would choose. In this section, Socrates antagonises the court even further when considering his proposition. He points out that the vote was comparatively close: Had only 30 more voted for him, he would have been found innocent. He engages in some dark humour by suggesting that Meletus be fined for not meeting the statutory one-fifth of the votes (in order to avoid frivolous cases coming to court, plaintiffs were fined heavily if the jurors' votes did not reach this number in a case where the defendant won). Assuming there were 501 or 500 jurymen, the prosecution had to gain at least 100 of the jurors' votes. Taken by itself, however, Meletus' vote (as representing one-third of the prosecution case) would have numbered only 93 or 94 (assuming 501 or 500 total jurors). Regardless of the number of plaintiffs, it was their case that had to reach the requisite one-fifth. Not only that, the prosecutors had won.

Socrates' next proposition most upset the jurors: As a benefactor to Athens, free meals in the Prytaneum, one of the important buildings which housed members of the Council. This was an honour reserved for athletes and other prominent citizens.

Finally, Socrates considers imprisonment and banishment before settling on a fine of 100 drachmae, as he had little funds of his own with which he could pay the fine. This was a small sum when weighed against the punishment proposed by the prosecutors and gave the jury little choice but to vote for the death penalty. Socrates' supporters immediately increased the amount to 3,000 drachmae, but in the eyes of the jury this was not an alternative. The jury decided on the sentence of death by drinking hemlock.

Plato indicates that the majority of jurors voted in favour of the death penalty, but he does not indicate exactly how many did. Our only source for the actual numbers of these votes is Diogenes Laertius, who says that 80 more voted for the death sentence than had voted for Socrates' guilt in the first place; but the details of this account have been disputed. Others have concluded from this that Socrates' speech angered the jury.

Socrates now responds to the verdict. He first addresses those who voted for death. He claims that it is not a lack of arguments that has resulted in his condemnation, but rather his unwillingness to stoop to the usual emotive appeals expected of any defendant facing death. Again he insists that the prospect of death does not absolve one from following the path of goodness and truth. Socrates prophesies that younger and harsher critics will follow him and submit them to an even more telling examination of their lives.

Socrates concludes his *Apology* with the claim that he bears no grudge against those who accused and condemned him, and asks them to look after his three sons as they grow up, ensuring that they put goodness before selfish interests.

O judges, be of good cheer about death, and know of a certainty, that no evil can happen to a good man, either in life or after death. He and his are not neglected by the gods; nor has my own approaching end happened by mere chance. But I see clearly that the time had arrived when it was better for me to die and be released from trouble. . . .

The hour of departure has arrived, and we go our separate ways, I to die, and you to live. Which of these two is better only God knows.

The Apology focuses more on Socrates' philosophical opinions, which, as he so persistently claims, are agnostic regarding any factual questions. Four philosophic points emerged out of *The Apology*.

1) The only true wisdom consists in knowing that you know nothing.

2) The improvement or "tendance" of the soul, the care for wisdom, and truth, is the highest good.

3) If you condemn me, you will sin against the gods who have given me to you.

4) Virtue is knowledge. To know the good is to do the good. "No one does evil voluntarily."

5) Socrates concludes by acknowledging that he does not, and cannot, know for certain what awaits him after death.

❑

The Individual and the State

Plato's description of Socrates' final days continued in the Crito (Κρι.των).

In prison, awaiting execution, Socrates displays the same spirit of calm reflection about serious matters that had characterized his life in freedom. Even the patent injustice of his fate at the hands of the Athenian jury produces in Socrates no bitterness or anger. Friends arrive at the jail with a foolproof plan for his escape from Athens to a life of voluntary exile, but Socrates calmly engages them in a rational debate about the moral value of such an action.

The *Crito* seems intended to exhibit the character of Socrates in one light only; not as the philosopher, fulfilling a divine mission and trusting in the will of heaven, but simply as the good citizen, who having been unjustly condemned is willing to give up his life in obedience to the laws of the state.

Not as the philosopher, fulfilling a divine mission and trusting in the will of heaven, but simply as the good citizen, who

having been unjustly condemned Socrates is willing to give up his life in obedience to the laws of the state.

The days of Socrates are drawing to a close; the fatal ship has been seen off Sunium (Σουτνιο), as he is informed by Crito, who visits him before the dawn has broken; he himself has been warned in a dream that on the third day he must depart. Time is precious, and Crito has come early in order to gain his consent to a plan of escape. This can be easily accomplished by his

Socrates teaching

friends, who will incur no danger in making the attempt to save him, but will be disgraced for ever if they allow him to perish. He should think of his duty to his children, and not play into the hands of his enemies. Money is already provided by Crito as well as by Simmias (Σιμμιας) of Thebes and others, and he will have no difficulty in finding friends in Thessaly (Θεσσαλι.α), a periphery of Greece.

Socrates is afraid that Crito is but pressing upon him the opinions of the many: whereas, all his life long he has followed the dictates of reason only and the opinion of the one wise or skilled man. There was a time when Crito himself had allowed the propriety of this. And although some one will say 'the many can kill us,' that makes no difference; but a good life, in other words, a just and honourable life, is alone to be valued. All considerations of loss of reputation or injury to his children should be dismissed: The only question is whether he would be right in attempting to escape.

Crito, who is a disinterested person, not having the fear of death before his eyes, shall answer this for him. Before he was condemned they had often held discussions, in which they agreed that no man should either do evil, or return evil for evil, or betray the right. Are these principles to be altered because the circumstances of Socrates are altered? Crito admits that they remain the same. Then is his escape consistent with the maintenance of them? To this Crito is unable or unwilling to reply.

Socrates proceeds: Suppose the Laws of Athens to come and remonstrate with him. They will ask 'Why does he seek to overturn them?' and if he replies, 'They have injured him,' will not the Laws answer, 'Yes, but was that the agreement?' Has he any objection to make to them which would justify him in overturning them? Was he not brought into the world and educated by their help, and are they not his parents? He might have left Athens and gone where he pleased, but he has lived there for seventy years more constantly than any other citizen.'

Thus he has clearly shown that he acknowledged the agreement, which he cannot now break without dishonour to himself and danger to his friends. Even in the course of the trial he might have proposed exile as the penalty, but then he declared that he preferred death to exile. And whither will he direct his footsteps?

In any well-ordered state the Laws will consider him as an enemy. Possibly in a land of misrule like Thessaly he may be welcomed at first, and the unseemly narrative of his escape will be regarded by the inhabitants as an amusing tale. But if he offends them he will have to learn another sort of lesson. Will he continue to give lectures in virtue? That would hardly be decent. And how will his children be the gainers if he takes them into Thessaly, and deprives them of Athenian citizenship? Or if he leaves them behind, does he expect that they will be better taken care of by his friends because he is in Thessaly? Will not true friends care for them equally whether he is alive or dead?

Finally, they exhort him to think of justice first, and of life and children afterwards. He may now depart in peace and innocence, a sufferer and not a doer of evil. But if he breaks agreements, and returns evil for evil, they will be angry with him while he lives; and their brethren the Laws of the world below will receive him as an enemy.

Such is the mystic voice which is always murmuring in his ears.

That Socrates was not a good citizen was a charge made against him during his lifetime, which has been often repeated in later ages. The crimes of Alcibiades, Critias, and Charmides, who had been his pupils, were still recent in the memory of the now restored democracy. The fact that he had been neutral in the death-struggle of Athens was not likely to conciliate popular good-will. Plato, writing probably in the next generation, undertakes the defence of his friend and master in this particular field, not to the Athenians of his day, but to posterity and the world at large.

Whether such an incident ever really occurred as the visit of Crito and the proposal of escape is uncertain. Plato could easily have invented far more than that; and in the selection of Crito, the aged friend, as the fittest person to make the proposal to Socrates, we seem to recognize the hand of the artist. Whether anyone who has been subjected by the laws of his country to an unjust judgment is right in attempting to escape, is a thesis about which casuists might disagree. Shelley (*Prose Works*) is of opinion that Socrates 'did well to die,' but not for the 'sophistical' reasons which Plato has put into his mouth. And there would be no difficulty in arguing that Socrates should have lived and preferred to a glorious death the good which he might still be able to perform. 'A rhetorician would have had much to say upon that point.' It may be observed however that Plato never intended to answer the question of casuistry, but only to exhibit the ideal of patient virtue which refuses to do the least evil in order to avoid the greatest, and to show his master maintaining in death the opinions which he had professed in his life. Not 'the world,' but the 'one wise man,' is still the paradox of Socrates in his last hours. He must be guided by reason, although her conclusions may be fatal to him. The remarkable sentiment that the wicked can do neither good nor evil is true, if taken in the sense, which he means, of moral evil; in his own words, 'they cannot make a man wise or foolish.'

This little dialogue is a perfect piece of dialectic, in which granting the 'common principle,' there is no escaping from the conclusion. It is anticipated at the beginning by the dream of Socrates and the parody of Homer. The personification of the Laws, and of their brethren the Laws in the world below, is one of the noblest and boldest figures of speech which occur in Plato.

Of course Crito and the others know their teacher well, and they come prepared to argue the merits of their plan. Escaping now would permit Socrates to fulfil his personal obligations in life. Moreover, if he does not follow the plan, many people will suppose that his friends did not care enough for him to arrange his escape. Therefore, in order to honour his commitments and preserve the reputation of his friends, Socrates ought to escape from jail.

But Socrates dismisses these considerations as irrelevant to a decision about what action is truly right. What other people will say clearly doesn't matter. As he had argued in the *Apology*, the only opinion that counts is not that of the majority of people generally, but rather that of the one individual who truly knows. The truth alone deserves to be the basis for decisions about human action, so the only proper approach is to engage in the

Socrates arguing with a sophist

sort of careful moral reasoning by means of which one may hope to reveal it.

The only opinion that counts is not that of the majority of people generally, but rather that of the one individual who truly knows.

The dialogue begins with Socrates waking up to the presence of Crito in his prison cell. Crito is a wealthy friend and disciple of Socrates. When Socrates expresses surprise that the guard has let him in at such an early hour, Crito informs Socrates that he knows the guard well and has done him a certain benefaction.

Crito has bad news for Socrates. He tells him that there are eyewitness reports that the ship has come in from Delos, and that tomorrow Socrates will be executed. Socrates rebuffs the report, saying he has had a dream—a vision of a woman in a white cloak telling him that on the third day hence he will go to Phthia, which is a reference to the Iliad. Socrates says that the meaning of this is perfectly clear—it will be three days until he dies.

Crito does not allow Socrates to elaborate the meaning of the dream, but only calls him daimonic; Crito has arrived at this early hour to save Socrates from death. Crito tells Socrates that if he follows through with the execution, people will assume that Crito and friends were too cheap to finance an escape. Crito's worries suggest that buying one's way out of prison was so common that people not only did not frown on it, but even expected it.

Socrates refuses Crito's initial offer to pay off potential snitches, and Crito protests that the informers are cheaply bought. He adds that if Socrates is afraid of depleting Crito's account, there are foreigners, Simmias and Cebes, who have come to town with money.

Crito then presents the moral view of the common man; a father has an obligation to nurture and educate his children, and should avoid orphaning them if at all possible. He tells Socrates that if his sons do not meet with the usual fate of orphans, it will be no thanks to him. Crito does not offer to see personally to the children's care, however. Crito adds that the trial should never have taken place and might have been managed differently. He says that the failure to escape will be a ridiculous climax to the whole affair, and caused by shameful cowardice of Socrates' friends.

Socrates tells Crito that he is one of those people who must be guided by reason. He expresses contempt for the opinions of the masses of mankind who think irrationally and act randomly. Socrates says that the only person whose opinion is of value is the one who understands justice. Money, reputation, and feeding children are values of thoughtless men. Socrates then invites Crito to consider the definition of justice, and whether it is ever right to do wrong intentionally.

Socrates takes the position that requiting injustice by retaliation or warding off evil by evil is always wrong, and is just as wrong as committing injustice in the first place. Socrates tells Crito that this opinion—that it is wrong not to resist evil—never has been, and never will be held by the vast majority of mankind. He thinks it is an important moral yardstick, adding that people who do not agree on this point have no common ground and must

Socrates and Alcibiades

necessarily despise each other. He says that this premise will be taken as true for the purpose of their discussion.

Crito says he agrees with Socrates that warding off evil by evil is as wrong as injustice, but in fact, neither seems to trouble him. Crito has no more qualms about bribing a friend's way out of prison than he had bribing his own way in for a morning visit. Neither man seems to notice that, according to Socrates, they should not even be friends because they are so far apart morally.

Resisting evil by any means other than persuasion is evil.

Socrates' claim that resisting evil by any means other than persuasion is evil is an ancient statement of moral pacifism. Socrates rests its logical defence entirely upon an analogy. He says that a citizen stands in relation to the state as the child does to the parent, as the slave does to his master. He says that the state has brought him into the world, by regulating marriage, nurtured, and educated him. Socrates says that he is the offspring and slave of the state and has no right to destroy the state by failing to obey it after it has been so beneficent to him.

❑

The Basis for Virtue

Plato's *Meno* (menõ) centres on the general problem of the origins of our moral knowledge. In a setting uncluttered by concern for Socrates' fate, it introduces some of the epistemological and metaphysical themes.

The Greek notion of virtue (arête) is that of an ability or skill in some particular respect. The virtue of a baker is what enables the baker to produce good bread; the virtue of the gardener is what enables the gardener to grow nice flowers; etc. In this sense, virtues clearly differ from person to person and from goal to goal. But Socrates is interested in true virtue, which like genuine health, should be the same for everyone. This broad concept of virtue may include such specific virtues as courage, wisdom, or moderation, but it should nevertheless be possible to offer a perfectly general description of virtue as a whole, the skill, or ability to be fully human. But what is that?

The dialogue begins with Meno asking Socrates to tell him if virtue can be taught. Socrates says that he is clueless about what virtue is, and so is everyone else he knows. Meno responds that virtue is different for different people, that what is virtuous for a man is to conduct himself in the city so that he helps his friends, injures his enemies, and takes care all the while that he personally comes to no harm. Virtue is different for a woman, he says. Her domain is the management of the household, and she is supposed to obey her husband. He says that children have their own proper virtue, and so do old men. Socrates says he finds this odd. He suspects that there must be some virtue common to all human beings.

Socrates rejects the idea that human virtue depends on a person's gender or age. He leads Meno towards the idea that virtues are common to all people, that temperance (sophrosunê-exercising self control) and justice (dikê, refraining from harming other people) are virtues even in children and old men.

Meno proposes that virtue is the desire for good things and the power to get them. Socrates points out that this raises a second problem- many people do not recognize evil. The discussion then turns to how to account for the fact that so many people are mistaken about good and evil, and take one for the other. Socrates asks Meno to consider whether good things must be acquired virtuously in order to be really good. Socrates leads onto the question of whether virtue is one thing or many.

No satisfactory definition of virtue emerges in the *Meno*. Socrates' comments, however, show that he considers a successful definition to be unitary, rather than a list of varieties of virtue, that it must contain all and only those terms which are genuine instances of virtue, and must not be circular.

When Meno suggests that virtue is simply the desire for good things, Socrates argues that this cannot be the case. Since different human beings are unequal in virtue, virtue must be something that varies among them, he argues, but desire for one believed to be good is perfectly universal. Since no human being ever knowingly desires what is bad, differences in their conduct must be a consequence of differences in what they know.

This is a remarkable claim.

Socrates holds that knowing what is right automatically results in the desire to do it; even though this feature of our moral experience could be doubted.

Since no human being ever knowingly desires what is bad, differences in their conduct must be a consequence of differences in what they know.

Wife, Xanthippe empties the chamber-pot over the head of Socrates

For questions of this sort, Socrates raises a serious dilemma: How can we ever learn what we do not know? Either we already know what we are looking for, in which case we do not need to look, or we do not know what we are looking for, in which case we would not recognize it if we found it. The paradox of knowledge is that, in the most fundamental questions about our own nature and function, it seems impossible for us to learn anything. The only escape, Socrates proposed, is to acknowledge that we already know what we need to know. This is the doctrine of recollection, a conviction that our most basic knowledge comes when we bring back to mind our acquaintance with eternal realities during a previous existence of the soul.

Socrates asks Meno if his slave boy speaks Greek, and when Meno assures him that he was born and bred in his household, Socrates begins one of the most influential dialogues of Western philosophy regarding the argument for innate knowledge. By drawing geometric figures in the ground Socrates demonstrates that the slave is initially unaware of how to find twice the area of a square.

After witnessing the example with the slave boy, Meno tells Socrates that he thinks that Socrates is correct in his theory of recollection, to which Socrates replies, "I think I am. I shouldn't like to take my oath on the whole story, but one thing I am ready to fight for as long as I can, in word and act—that is, that we shall be better, braver, and more active men if we believe it right to look for what we don't know."

We shall be better, braver, and more active men if we believe it right to look for what we do not know.

In an interesting interlude, Socrates praises Anytus, son of Anthemion, who earned his fortune with intelligence and hard work. He says that Anthemion had his son well-educated, and Anytus, the beneficiary of a well-meaning father, must both be virtuous and know what it is. Anytus disagrees. Socrates then questions why it is that men do not always produce sons of the same virtue as themselves. He alludes to other notable male figures, such as Themistocles, Aristides, Pericles, and Thucydides, and casts doubt on whether these men produced sons as capable of virtue as themselves. Anytus becomes offended and accuses Socrates of slander, warning him to be careful while expressing such opinions. Socrates suggests that Anytus does not realize what slander is, and continues his dialogue with Meno as to the definition of Virtue.

Socrates points out the similarities and differences between "true beliefs" and "knowledge". He claims that while "true beliefs" may be as useful to us as knowledge, they often fail to "stay in their place" and must be "tethered" by anamnesis. This distinction between "true beliefs" and "knowledge" forms the basis of the philosophical definition of knowledge as "justified true belief". "To sum up our enquiry," Socrates concludes, "the result seems to be, if we are at all right in our view, that virtue is neither natural nor acquired, but an instinct given by God to the virtuous."

Using an interesting analogy, Socrates points out that we use the term bee in the singular to describe a host of different animals. Real living bees are all different from each other, but we recognize that they are all bees. Hence, there must be some concept, some idea, or some form in common, which they all share and by virtue of which they are all bees and through which we can classify a particular flying insect as a bee or not. There is no single living bee which defines the species. The species bee is an idea, or to introduce a term we are using now and then, it is a universal. We cannot see it out there in the garden buzzing around the flowers, but we can apprehend it in our minds.

In the remainder of the discussion, Socrates and Meno discuss whether virtue meets this criterion of knowledge, and they come to the conclusion that virtue is not being taught, since there are no teachers and no pupils. Even those men most eminent for their virtue in Athens were unable to educate their children. Hence, they arrive at the unacceptably paradoxical conclusion that virtue is a gift from the gods and that those who possess it in this way have no knowledge of virtue. And that, Socrates concludes, is all we can say about the issue at the moment.

This ending is inconclusive and paradoxical, but the implications of where we ought to go from here to address our residual doubts are clear enough. Socrates has made a case for his faith in the search for universals as the basis for knowledge and on the appropriate method for seeking them out. He has not proved anything conclusively, but he has issued a challenge for those who want to base their lives on more than simply received opinion or to accept the disagreeable consequence of cultural and moral relativism and indicated a direction we should follow.

Socrates is not proposing that we determine our own truths and live by them. The opposite is here the case. If we are ever to understand virtue, we must see it as something universal, something ideal which includes and helps to define all the specific acts of virtue in the lives around us, something as convincing to each and every one of us as a geometrical demonstration. Our understanding of virtue must be grounded in that same certainty of knowledge. That is the challenge he leaves us with at the conclusion of the dialogue.

Socrates is revolutionary in his critical stance towards his community's traditions. Whether we know anything about the content of what he is proposing, he stands as the most famous of all those who demand that long-standing traditions answer to a new standard, something which exists above and beyond the values and habits of the community, unless those values and habits can be justified by an appeal to the Truth, a concept which they do not define but to which they must answer if we are to accept them as a guide for the good life.

Unlike Moses, whose chief concern is to discipline his people into following a shared tradition because it comes from God, and that is all there is to it, and unlike Oedipus, who defines his excellence in terms the community recognizes, or

Gilgamesh, who comes through to appreciate through experience the traditional values of his community, Socrates is insisting on a new, rational standard. He, thus, stands as the natural inspirer of all those who wish to challenge inherited moralities in the name of reason.

Socrates stands as the natural inspirer of all those who wish to challenge inherited moralities in the name of reason.

At the heart of the new challenge is the rational search for universal truths. These universal truths exist as a standard against which we measure truth claims and differentiate them from opinions, (no matter how useful such opinions might be), because such universals are grounded. We do not create them for ourselves. Through a process of conversational enquiry we discover them, and because they are based on truths knowable by all human beings, they can be taught in a way that transcends the variety of cultural traditions and beliefs. A major task of our moral life becomes thinking our way through beliefs posing as knowledge claims.

Socrates dramatically changes the nature of our enquiries. After Socrates, one cannot discuss questions of virtue without raising the issue of knowledge, and one cannot put that into the discussion without addressing the question of universals, innate ideas, the appropriate method for discovering these ideas, and the language appropriate for that enquiry.

A universal, unambiguously employed, signifies something or it does not. If it signifies anything, that something is not an arbitrary fiction of my mind; if it signifies nothing, there is an end of all science. Science stands or falls with "objective reference." In ethics the doctrine means that there really is one moral standard for all of us, male or female, civilized or barbarian, bound or free. There really is one "eternal and immutable" morality, not a variety of independent moral standards, one perhaps for the "private man" and another for the "nation" or its politicians, or one for "the followers" and another for the "leader."

Socrates is not answering in Meno or elsewhere these complex issues. He is inviting us to a life in which we join in an ongoing conversation to explore where such considerations take us. The virtue lies in the process, not in the destination—at least that is his hope. The search for truth is to be valued above the search for material success.

❑

Immortality of the Soul

The Phaedo (Φαι.δων) concludes Plato's description of the life of Socrates. He has spent a rather long time in jail after the trial described in the Apology, in which he was condemned to death by the "men of Athens." Now, he is here in company with devoted, if dogmatic, friends, whom he addresses as "judges". What statement must he defend? The philosopher must be willing to die readily. How can he be so calm? We remember the "Socratic ignorance" displayed in the *Apology*. Socrates will never say flat out that he knows what awaits him in death. He never makes knowledge-claims, we might say, but he tells stories. He does not insist but he "expects."

The dialogue is told by memory by Phaedo to Echecrates. The main theme in the *Phaedo* is the idea that the soul is immortal. Socrates offers four arguments for the soul's immortality: Cyclical argument, the theory of recollection, the affinity argument, and the argument of form of Life.

The cyclical argument, or argument of opposites, explains that as the forms are eternal and unchanging, and as the soul always brings life, and then it must not die, and is necessarily imperishable. As the body is mortal and is subject to physical death, the soul must be its indestructible opposite. Socrates then suggests the analogy of fire and cold. If the form of cold is imperishable, and fire, its opposite, was within close proximity, it would have to withdraw intact as does the soul during death. This could be likened to the idea of the opposite charges of magnets.

The theory of recollection explains that we possess some non-empirical knowledge at birth, implying the soul existed before birth to carry that knowledge.

The affinity argument explains that invisible, immortal, and incorporeal things are different from visible, mortal, and corporeal things. Our soul is of the former, while our body is of the latter, so when our bodies die and decay, our soul will continue to live.

The argument of form of life explains that the forms, incorporeal and static entities, are the cause of all things in the world, and all things participate in forms. For example, beautiful things participate in the form of beauty; the number four participates in the form of the even, etc. The soul, by its very nature, participates in the form of life, which would mean the soul could never die.

What happens when we die, after all, is that the human soul separates from the human body, and it is concern for the soul rather than the body that characterizes a philosophical life. Since knowledge of the most important matters in life is clearest to the soul alone, its customary attachment to a mortal body often serves only as a distraction from what counts. We get hungry or sleepy, and the needs of the body interfere with our work. We may therefore be proper in looking forward to death as a release from bodily limitations. But is there really any reason to believe that the soul can continue to exist and function after the body dies? The arguments on this point occupy the bulk of the *Phaedo*.

The first argument is based on the cyclical interchange by means of which every quality comes into being from its own opposite. Hot comes from cold and cold from hot: That is, hot things are just cold things that have warmed up, and cold things are just hot things that have cooled off. Similarly, people who are awake are just people who were asleep but then woke up, while people who are asleep are just people who were awake but then dozed off.

But then, by analogy, death must come from life and life from death. That is, people who are dead are just people who were alive but then experienced the transition we call dying, and people who are alive are just people who were among the dead but then experienced the transition we call being born. This suggests a perpetual recycling of human souls from the realm of the living to the realm of the dead and back.

If this is an accurate image of reality, it would certainly follow that my soul will continue to exist after the death of my body. But it also supposes that my soul existed before the birth of my body as well. This may seem like an extravagant speculation, but Socrates argues that there is ample evidence of its truth in the course of ordinary human life and learning.

As Socrates had proposed in the Meno, the most important varieties of human knowledge are really cases of recollection. Consider, for example, our knowledge of equality. We have no difficulty in deciding whether or not two people are perfectly equal in height. In fact, they are never exactly the same height, since we recognize that it would always be possible to discover some difference—however minute—with a more careful, precise measurement. By this standard, all of the examples we perceive in ordinary life only approach, but never fully attain, perfect equality. But notice that since we realize the truth of this important qualification on our experience, we must somehow know for sure what true equality is, even though we have never seen it.

Socrates in Athens

The same point could be made with regard to many other abstract concepts: Even though we perceive only their imperfect instances, we have genuine knowledge of truth, goodness, and beauty no less than of equality. Things of this sort are indeed forms, abstract entities that exist independently of the sensible world. Ordinary objects are imperfect and changeable, but they faintly copy the perfect and immutable forms. Thus, all of the information we acquire about sensible objects, like knowing what the high and low temperatures were yesterday, is temporary, insignificant, and unreliable, while genuine knowledge of the forms themselves, like knowing that 93 - 67 = 26, is perfectly certain forever.

Since we really do have knowledge of these supra-sensible realities, knowledge that we cannot possibly have obtained through any bodily experience must be a form of recollection; the experiences that our souls must have been acquainted with the forms prior to our births. In that case, the existence of our mortal bodies cannot be essential to the existence of our souls—before birth or after death—and we are therefore immortal.

Use of the dialogue as a literary device made it easy to present one position, in the voice of Socrates, but also to consider, in the voices of other characters, significant objections that might be raised against it. This does not mean that philosophy is merely an idle game of argument and counter-argument, Socrates pointed out, because it remains our goal to discover the one line of argument that leads to the truth. The philosopher cautiously investigates every possibility and examines every side of an issue, precisely because that increases the chances of arriving eventually at a correct account of reality.

Thus, Simmias (Σιμμι.ας) of Thebes suggests that the relationship between the soul and the body may be like that between musical harmony and the strings of a lyre that produces it. In this case, even though the soul is significantly different from the body, it could not reasonably be expected to survive the utter destruction of that physical thing. This is an early statement of a view of human nature that would later come to be called epiphenomenalism. But Socrates replies that this analogy will not hold, since the soul exercises direct control over the motions of the body, while the harmony does not have any control over the strings of the lyre. Plato's suggestion here seems to be that it would become impossible to provide an adequate account of human morality, of the proper standards for acting rightly, if Simmias were right.

Cebes of Thebes is represented as an earnest seeker after virtue and truth, keen in argument and cautious in decision. Cebes offers a more difficult objection: what if the body is like a garment worn by the soul? Even though I continue to exist longer than any single article of my clothing does, there will come a time when I die, and some of my clothes will probably continue to exist. In the same way, even if the argument from opposites has shown that the soul can in principle outlast the life of any particular human body, there might come a time when the soul itself ceases to exist. Even if there is life after death, Cebes suggests, the soul may not be truly immortal.

Cebes demands a complete investigation of the causes of genesis and destruction. Socrates will tell his experiences here: when he was young, he was wondrously lustful about knowledge of nature. But he convinced himself he had no nature for this kind of investigation. But then he came across writings of Anaxagoras, who claims mind is arranger of all and cause of what is best, so we should study mind as the best. The true cause of Socrates being in jail is that the Athenians thought it best that he be there; it would be absurd to focus on Socrates' body, the material cause of his being there, as a true cause in this case. Socrates demands that we distinguish the cause and the pre-conditions, and then claims that it is "the good" which holds everything together.

In response to this criticism, Socrates significantly revised the argument from opposites by incorporating an additional conception of the role of the forms. Each form, he now maintains, is the cause of all of every particular instance that bears its name: the form of beauty causes the beauty of any beautiful thing; the form of equality causes the equality of any pair of equal things; etc. But then, since the soul is living, it must participate in the Form of Life, and thus it cannot ever die. The soul is perfectly and certainly imperishable, not only for this life, but forever.

Wishing to avoid the blindness of those who look at the sun, he looks instead at its image in water. This is itself an image of his philosophical method: instead of looking at things in themselves with his eyes, he looks at their truth in logos (λογοττυπος) or symbol or image. But, he warns, be careful with this image. This is vitally important: there are images in everyday interaction with things, in our primary looking at and dealing with things. The philosopher is the one who knows that even the everyday is imagistic, that recognizes the social/historical constitution of everyday "reality." Rather than risk the soul-blindness of unexamined everyday life, the philosopher recognizes the inescapable mediation of perception by culture, as Socrates makes clear next.

There are images in everyday interaction with things. The philosopher is the one who recognizes the social/historical constitution of everyday "reality."

Recognizing the necessity of logos and hypothesis, Socrates puts himself in an infinite process of self-critique through exposure to others; his positions can be nothing other than temporary and imperfect, and the best positions are those arrived at through widest possible exposure to others. Here we see the bizarre sight of a democratic Socrates: the more a polis allowed as many as possible to achieve their natures the more sure the philosophers would be that they were on the right track.

Despite the apparent force of these logical arguments, the *Phaedo* is concluded presenting a mythical image of life after death. This concrete picture of the existence of a world beyond our own is imagined, not reasoned, so it cannot promise to deliver the same perfect representation of the truth. Even if we are not fully convinced by the certainty of rational arguments, we may yet take some comfort from the suggestions of a pleasant story.

❑

The Relevance of Socrates

Socrates' thinking and his life was characterized by doing philosophy and pursuing knowledge. For Socrates this meant questioning those who claimed to know something. This in turn generated a lot of enmity towards him and he was put on trial, convicted, and sentenced to death for refusing to stop criticizing and discrediting those who had power and influence in Athens.

This book encourages anyone who does not know Socrates, his story and his ideas, the account of his defence against the false charges which were brought against him and his justification for pursuing philosophy and living the kind of life that he did. This concluding chapter briefly discuss some of the most valuable insights of Socrates.

Socrates is after knowledge but he is very careful about the claims that he makes. He says that he knows nothing, and that unlike sophists, he does not have any wisdom worth selling. But he does sometimes make some strong claims about those things that are important to him and which he considers to be most worthy and valuable. Socrates' main advice in the Apology and his philosophical mission is the care of the soul. He urges every

Athenian and anyone who wants to listen to him to not go after money, fame, or possessions but to take every care of the soul and make it as good as possible. Socrates believes that the former things are not so worthy and that the way to care for the soul is by pursuing virtues. But what is pursuing virtues?

Socrates urges anyone who wants to listen to him to not go after money, fame, or possessions but to take every care of the soul and make it as good as possible.

In the ancient Greek world, the word for virtue was arête and it referred to excellence of any kind. Virtues are achieved and exercised in the course of those human activities in which pursuing and excelling in them brings with it some additional virtues, good effects and benefits that can only be found in those activities or activities like them.

While kicking a ball well is not a form of activity and an arena in which virtues are exhibited, the game of football is because in becoming good at it, one also learns, for instance, about team play and working in unison with others, about fair play, respect and playing by the rules, and working towards accomplishing short and long term goals. Moreover, acquiring these good qualities is part of what makes the game what it is, and if a person tries to get around them, then he or she just cannot be a good player.

Bricklaying is not an activity in which virtues can be exhibited and cultivated, but architecture is. The virtues can also be exercised in pursuing a wide range of activities because there are all kinds of side benefits and good rewards in pursuing arts, music, philosophy, mathematics, sciences, law, writing, and so nowhere you are not only excelling in what you are doing but are also becoming good at other things and in other ways. Of course in pursuing these activities, one can end up with prestige, social status, and money, but what connects them with virtues are not these external goods but picking up the virtues—the abilities, qualities, and insights—which can only be gained by excelling in them. In doing philosophy and pursuing knowledge by studying many thinkers over many years, one not only learns about philosophy and how to test knowledge claims, but one is also likely to become better at listening to others, more willing to contemplate views that are different from one's own, more civil and polite, and better in expressing oneself clearly and thinking clearly, more charitable to other people's views, and so on.

What is important to note is that the external goods that come with pursuing some complex activities, such as wealth and good jobs, are scarce, there is often competition over them, and there are sometimes winners and losers, but the internal goods, the virtues that Socrates takes to be the worthy things, are always free, plenty and available for anyone who wants to pursue them, with enough left for others. Moreover, pursuing them not only makes you better but it brings benefits to those around you. It is even possible that we pursue excellence in some activity and never become very good at it, but still walk away with some

Death of Socrates

other virtues and abilities. So there are even rewards for not very good football players and students of philosophy. However, needless to say, most people often have their eyes on the external goods and see complex human activities and endeavours as a means to them and very often there are few takers when it comes to the virtues.

This conception of virtue and excellence which I have been describing is not very well-known and prominent in the contemporary world. It is an important part of Socrates' thinking on Ethics. What is unique about it is that it is about focusing on making oneself good. It is about putting pressure and being hard on one's own self. It is about working on cultivating and creating the self. To pursue the virtues, you need to understand them and have a clear account of them. You must have a sharp eye on them. But you also crucially need a conception of yourself as one who desires them but lacks them and a conception of yourself as one who possess them and is empowered by them, so that you can work your way from the former state to the latter. In other words, to reach your potential and become good, you need a conception of yourself as who you are and a conception of yourself based on who you can be, so that you can realize it and move towards that end.

This conception of what it means to be good is very different than the kind of popular, cheap, and easy morality which comes from having your eyes on the supposed sins of others and from judging others quickly and harshly. Socrates was convicted and put to death largely because of the terrible but false things that were said about him by those who listen, add to, and spread this kind of stuff. Clearly, those who are always talking about the faults of others, those who are perpetually in the state of shock over the supposed bad behaviours and actions of others, and those who can only feel good about themselves by bringing others down, do not know about the virtues and the way of virtues. Those who, like mullahs, normalize others and are punishers are often so sure of their own righteousness that they hardly worry about their own moral blind spots and inadequacies or making themselves better. The virtues in contrast give us the knowledge of what to do, how to order our soul, how to become good, and how to achieve happiness, but not how to judge others.

What others make of themselves is of course largely their business and beyond our reach, but we have so much power over our own lives and what we can do with them and with ourselves. We really do not worry about the wrong things that other people do. We largely give them a free pass and expect nothing much of them, but we take responsibility for our own actions and keep a close eye on them. This is hardly missed on those who know me well. We also hate gossip and we often tell others that we do not consider wrong anything that consenting adults may do and that we are not interested in hearing about such things. Needless to say, we can not get into other people's minds and compel them to interpret this in a charitable way and not to turn into it something nasty and immoral, to be used against us. But even in those cases, our attitude is: go ahead and be our guest, if you must. Reader, truly, if you were to wrong us, we would of course not like it, but I would not dwell on it much because what you do simply does not fall under what we are responsible for.

Pursuing the virtues offers us a way to become good and to define ourselves based on what we achieve and accomplish and make of ourselves. This is in contrast to the conventional morality which often involves the making of the 'Other' and projecting the worst on those who are worse off than us, those who threaten us in some way and who we take to be our opponents, and bestowing high and good motives and instincts on ourselves. Sadly, we are usually very dismissive of others and the virtues of others because if we acknowledged that they had something over us, then we would have to stop what we are doing and address this lack. If we overlook the various virtues and the silent but strong demands that they make on us, then we can somehow go on being better and with peace pursue the external goods that we know of, like wealth and prestige. It is no wonder that Socrates believes that a life without examination is not worth living, we are simply unlikely to hit on some of the worthy things in life, unless we are searching for them in a focused and spirited manner.

The other insight from Socrates has to do with the Socratic Method. Socrates often uses dialogue and questioning to examine the definition and the nature of moral concepts such as piety, justice, temperance, courage, and virtue. I think that there is broad agreement that Socrates uses it in a negative way to show that the claims to know these things are false. Socrates often finds himself in the company of people who claim to know these moral concepts and to be able to give a definition of them, but he always manages to show that they have not pinned it down so well and that these definitions leave out important uses of the terms and considerations. Clearly, Socrates believes that when it comes to moral terms, there are no essences and no final and concrete definitions. Perhaps he wants us to reflect on how

Socrates conversing with a Muse

little we know and recognize our limitations as the first step in studying philosophy and pursuing knowledge.

Some thinkers assume that the only insight here is about scepticism about definitions and essences. But I think that there is more to the search for moral definitions than that. When we look closely at various perspectives on those concepts that form the basis of the moral life and reason about them, we can actually learn a lot about them, orient ourselves differently, and perhaps even become better human beings.

The Socratic cross-examination can strengthen and clarify our moral thinking in a number of ways. When we apply it to our own beliefs and compel ourselves to give good justifications for them, it makes us look at the assumptions behind our own ways of thinking, actions, and feelings. It can flush out some of the inconsistencies in our moral beliefs. This kind of self-examination can also compel us to order our moral life better and to better match our actions with our words. Those who do not have their moral values and beliefs in order and have not put their beliefs under examination, are probably confused about the right way to live and to act, have inconsistent moral views, practice self-deception more than others, and often act in a self-serving way. They may do whatever suits them, and later rationalize these actions in some way.

Reasoning about morality and looking closely at various views on morality and moral concepts can broaden our moral horizons. Socrates does not believe that right and wrong are merely matters of opinion and he opposes the moral relativism of the Sophists. But he believes that there are no simple definitions or essences for moral concepts. This however does not mean that the search for their meaning and looking at their nature closely is useless and a waste of time. Examining the various views on moral concepts can certainly help us to clarify them and come to a better understanding of them. It can help us with discovering the contours of these concepts, gradually unfolding them. We will not get crystal clear answers but things will become clearer. This investigation can also help us in coming up with more objective and impartial moral standards.

The ethical insights of Socrates remain as powerful and useful today as they have always been. Socrates like other philosophers is calling on us to listen to what he has to say and to reflect on these things. But if we do not have the ear for it, we will not hear him. Socrates was wise and had many insights, but this was missed by the Athenians. His wisdom was not beaming out of him and it was not easy to recognize. It required listening closely and charitably. Some found him and his mannerisms to be repulsive and perceived him as some kind of a threat because his questioning made them uneasy. He was not heard by them but made into a caricature.

But Plato listened to him with generosity. He believed that Socrates was a good man with a noble mission who was falsely charged with harming people. He knew what kind of a person Socrates was and he knew that the charges against him were false. Plato knew that Socrates would rather be harmed by others than inflict harm on them.

What is important to note here is that the good human qualities, such as fairness, understanding, self-command, and consideration for others must be cultivated and worked on, because we are unlikely to hit on them by chance or just pick them up casually. This is why philosophy and the search for values and answers are so important. The virtues are free for taking. They are right there next to us, they are in some sense near us, like on the mantle or on the bookcase, but we must first see them and recognize them, and then work hard to cultivate them to make them ours.

It is very difficult to turn people away from consoling themselves by comparing themselves with others and to compel them to be self critical and hard on themselves. People often just do not want to hear it. But undoubtedly this is the way to grow as a human being, to become mentally strong, to gain confidence in your self, and to become better. Morality is not about shaking your fingers at others, it is about serious and deep reflections on what sort of a person one is and turning oneself around.

Finally, for Socrates pursuing philosophy meant that he did not align himself with the powers to be or with the Athenian people, in the sense that he did not pander to them and extol their virtues. He did not think that rationalizing what the people do and believe is doing philosophy. He questioned authority and the establishment. He was also critical of easy answers. He believed

I know that I am intelligent, because I know that I know nothing."
—Socrates (470 - 399 BC)

that there are deeper truths and realities behind the appearances and he tried to get at them. He also encouraged those who would listen to him to search things out for themselves, using his question and answer method. This method was designed to help us to think for ourselves. To conform, to passively sacrifice our identity to society, and to submit to the majority may have their rewards but they can also mean not searching for and discovering higher and better things for our own selves. Socrates was worried about his own children becoming a part of the mass and asked others to not let this happen to them. This was one of his final wishes.

The importance of Socrates, like the importance of all great thinkers, is not that he gives us a neatly worked out answer. His importance stems from the nature of his questions, from the direction he points toward and the vocabulary he introduces into our conversations. Anyone who is always ready to toss out a thinker's efforts, including his assumptions and his method, because of some perceived inadequacy in the answer is not going to get very far in understanding any complex thinker.

Socrates, in fact and in effect, is inviting us to participate in a quest—not to repose in the cosy certainty of a received answer. The last thing he would want is for us to applaud him and believe that he has said all that needs to be said.

❑

Wisdom of Socrates

Action

Action or passion. It does not become because it is becoming.

Every action has its pleasures and its prices.

Admit

Admitting one's ignorance is the first step in acquiring knowledge.

Advice

My advice to you is get married: if you find a good wife you'll be happy; if not, you'll become a philosopher.

Age

I would be more embarrassed to be ignorant in my old age.

Alone

I alone know I am wise because I alone know I know nothing.

Alphabet

The alphabet will create forgetfulness in the learners' souls. They will trust the written characters and not remember themselves.

Ancient

I pity those reviewers above, and people like them, who ridicule authors like R.A. Boulay and other proponents of similar Ancient Astronaut theories, simply for putting forth so many interesting questions (because that's really what he often throughout openly admits is all he does) in light of fascinating and thought-provoking references which are all from copious sources.

Angers

Do not do to others what angers you if done to you by others.

Angry

Do not be angry with me if I tell you the truth.

Answer

The answer I gave myself and the oracle was that it was to my advantage to be as I am.

Antiphon

Antiphon, as another man gets pleasure from a good horse, or a dog, or a bird, I get even more pleasure from good friends. And if I have something good, I teach it to them, and I introduce them to others who will be useful to them with respect to virtue. And together with my friends I go through the treasures of wise men of old which they left behind written in books, and we peruse them. If we see something good, we pick it out and hold it to be a great profit, if we are able to prove useful to one another.

Army

A disorderly mob is no more an army than a heap of building materials is a house.

Art

Be slow to fall into friendship; but when thou art in, continue firm and constant.

Well, my art of midwifery is in most respects like theirs; but differs, in that I attend men and not women; and look after their souls when they are in labour, and not after their bodies: and the triumph of my art is in thoroughly examining whether the thought which the mind of the young man brings forth is a false idol or a noble and true birth. And like the mid-wives, I am barren, and the reproach which is often made against me, that I ask questions of others and have not the wit to answer them myself, is very just-the reason is, that the god compels-me to be a midwife, but does not allow me to bring forth. And therefore I am not myself at all wise, nor have I anything to show which is the invention or birth of my own soul, but those who converse with me profit.

Artisan

I went to the artisans, for I was conscious that I knew nothing at all, as I may say, and I was sure that they knew many fine things of which I was ignorant, and in this they certainly were wiser than I was. But I observed that even the good artisans fell into the same error as the poets; because they were good workmen they thought they knew all sorts of high matters, and this defect in them overshadowed their wisdom — therefore I asked myself on behalf of the oracle, whether I would like to be as I was, neither having their knowledge nor their ignorance, or like them in both; and I made answer to myself and the oracle that I was better off as I was.

Assign

If I can assign names as well as pictures to objects, the right assignment of them we may call truth, and the wrong assignment of them falsehood.

Athen

So now, Athenian men, more than on my own behalf must I defend myself, as some may think, but on your behalf, so that you may not make a mistake concerning the gift of god by condemning me. For if you kill me, you will not easily find another such person at all, even if to say in a ludicrous way, attached on the city by the god, like on a large and well-bred horse, by its size and laziness both needing arousing by some gadfly; in this way the god seems to have fastened me on the city, some such one who arousing and persuading and reproaching each one of you I do not stop the whole day settling down all over. Thus such another will not easily come to you, men, but if you believe me, you will spare me; but perhaps you might possibly be offended, like the sleeping who are awakened, striking me, believing Anytus, you might easily kill, then the rest of your lives you might continue sleeping, unless the god caring for you should send you another.

Could I climb the highest place in Athens, I would lift up my voice and proclaim, Fellow citizens, why do you burn and scrape every stone to gather wealth, and talk so little care of your children to whom you must one day relinquish all?

If I had engaged in politics, O men of Athens, I should have perished long ago, and done no good either to you or to myself.

Men of Athens, I honour and love you; but I shall obey God rather than you, and while I have life and strength I shall never cease from the practice and teaching of philosophy.

Athletics

Athletics have become professionalized.

Author

The author clearly cites all his fascinating sources and cross-references them rather plausibly. He organizes the information in a sequential manner that piques ones interest even as he jumps from one set of information to the next.

Authority

Whatever authority I may have rests solely on knowing how little I know.

Awareness

Awareness of ignorance is the beginning of wisdom.

Battle

Be nicer than necessary to everyone you meet. Everyone is fighting some kind of battle.

Beautiful

We do not know neither the sophists, nor the orators, nor the artists, nor I— what the True, the Good, and the Beautiful are. But there is this difference between us: although these people know nothing, they all believe they know something; whereas, I, if I know nothing, at least have no doubts about it. As a result, all this superiority in wisdom which the oracle has attributed to me reduces itself to the single point that I am strongly convinced that I am ignorant of what I do not know.

Beauty

Beauty comes first. Victory is secondary. What matters is joy.

Beauty is a short lived tyranny.

Beauty is the bait which with delight allures man to enlarge his kind.

By means of beauty all beautiful things become beautiful. For this appears to me the safest answer to give both to myself and others; and adhering to this, I think that I shall never fall, but that it is a safe answer both for me and anyone else to give — that by means of beauty beautiful things become beautiful.

By means of beauty, all beautiful things become beautiful.

Give me beauty in the inward soul; may the outward and the inward man be at one.

If there is anything beautiful other than absolute beauty, that can only be beautiful as far as it partakes of absolute beauty— and this I should say of everything, by beauty all things become beautiful, by greatness only great things become great and greater and greater, and by smallness the less becomes less.

Begin

All thinking begins with wondering.

Beginning

The beginning is the most important part, especially when dealing with anything young and tender.

The beginning of wisdom is the definition of terms.

Belief

My belief is that to have no wants is divine.

Believe

The uninitiated are those who believe in nothing except what they can grasp in their hands, and who deny the existence of all that is invisible.

To Believe without evidence and demonstration is an act of ignorance and folly.

When you propose ridiculous things to believe, too many men will choose to believe nothing at all.

I believe that we cannot live better than in seeking to become better, nor more agreeably than having a clear conscience.

I do believe that there are gods, and in a far higher sense than that in which any of my accusers believe in them.

I know you won't believe me, but the highest form of Human Excellence is to question oneself and others.

Best

It is best and easiest not to discredit others but to prepare oneself to be as good as possible.

It may be said, indeed, that without bones and muscles and the other parts of the body I cannot execute my purposes. But to say that I do as I do because of them, and that this is the way in which the mind acts, and not from the choice of the best, is a very careless and idle mode of speaking. I wonder that they cannot distinguish the cause from the condition, which the many, feeling about in the dark, are always mistaking and misnaming.

The best seasoning for food in hunger; for drink, thirst.

I have found the best way to give advice to your children is to find out what they want and then advise them to do it.

Better

Is it not, then, better to be ridiculous and friendly than clever and hostile?

It is better to be at odds with the whole world than, being one, to be at odds with myself.

It is better to change an opinion than to persist in a wrong one.

It is better to make a mistake with full force of your being than to carefully avoid mistakes with a trembling spirit.

It is better to suffer an injustice than to commit one.

It is better to suffer wrong than to do wrong.

Better to do a little well, then a great deal badly.

Blossom

Though flattery blossoms like friendship, yet there is a vast difference in the fruit.

Body

We can do nothing without the body, let us always take care that it is in the best condition to sustain us.

Who knows if to live is to be dead, and to be dead, to live? And we really, it may be, are dead; in fact I once heard sages say that we are now dead, and the body is our tomb.

Whoever would have his body supple, easy and healthful should learn to dance.

Besides, it is a shame to let yourself grow old through neglect before seeing how you can develop the maximum beauty and strength of body; and you can have this experience if your are negligent, because these things don't normally happen by themselves.

Either knowledge is not to be attained at all, or if at all, after death. For then and not till then, the soul will be in herself alone and without the body.

The body cannot be cured without regard for the soul.

The body is a source of endless trouble to us by reason of the mere requirement of food; and is also liable to diseases which overtake and impede us in the search after truth: and by filling us so full of loves, and lusts, and fears, and fancies, and idols, and every sort of folly, prevents our ever having, as people say, so much as a thought.

There is no illness of the body except for the mind.

Born

We admitted that everything living is born of the dead. For if the soul existed before birth, and in coming to life and being born can be born only from death and dying, must she not after death continue to exist, since she has to be born again?

Call

I call myself a Peaceful Warrior because the battles we fight are on the inside.

I call that man idle who might be better employed.

Care

I don't care what people say about me. I do care about my mistakes.

They who have a care of their souls, and do not merely live in the fashions of the body, say farewell to all this; they will not walk in the ways of the blind: and when philosophy offers them purification and release from evil, they feel that they ought not resist her influence, and to her they incline, and whither she leads they follow her.

Sometimes you put walls up not to keep people out, but to see who cares enough to break them down.

Certain

To be uncertain is to be uncomfortable, but to be certain is to be ridiculous.

Change

Do not grieve over someone who changes all of the sudden. It might be that he has given up acting and returned to his true self.

Only the extremely ignorant or the extremely intelligent can resist change.

Cheer

And I say let a man be of good cheer about his soul. When the soul has been arrayed in her own proper jewels temperance and justice, and courage, and nobility and truth - she is ready to go on her journey when the hour comes.

Let a man be of good cheer about his soul, who has cast away the pleasures and ornaments of the body as alien to him, and rather hurtful in their effects, and has followed after the pleasures of knowledge in this life; who has adorned the soul in her own proper jewels, which are temperance, and justice, and courage, and nobility, and truth—in these arrayed she is ready to go on her journey to the world below, when her time comes. You, Simmias and Cebes, and all other men, will depart at some time or other. Me already, as the tragic poet would say, the voice of fate calls.

Child

We can easily forgive a child who is afraid of the dark; the real tragedy of life is when men are afraid of the light.

Children

Children today are tyrants. They contradict their parents, gobble their food, and tyrannize their teachers.

The children now love luxury; they have bad manners, contempt for authority; they show disrespect for elders and love chatter in place of exercise. Children are now tyrants, not the servants of their households. They no longer rise when elders enter the room. They contradict their parents, chatter before company, gobble up dainties at the table, cross their legs, and tyrannize their teachers.

Choice

Do we have no choice but to agree that in each of us are found the same elements and characteristics as are found in the city? After all, where else could the city have got them from?

Citizen

I am a citizen of the world, and my nationality is goodwill.

I am a citizen, not of Athens, or Greece, but of the world.

I am not an Athenian or a Greek, but a citizen of the world.

City

I was attached to this city by the god—though it seems a ridiculous thing to say—as upon a great and noble horse which was somewhat sluggish because of its size and needed to be stirred up by a kind of gadfly. It is to fulfil some such function that I believe the god has placed me in the city. I never cease to rouse each and every one of you, to persuade and reproach you.

Coin

Is there not one true coin for which all things ought to exchange?- and that is wisdom; and only in exchange for this, and in company with this, is anything truly bought or sold, whether courage, temperance or justice. And is not all true virtue the companion of wisdom, no matter what fears or pleasures or other similar goods or evils may or may not attend her? But the virtue which is made up of these goods, when they are severed from wisdom and exchanged with one another, is a shadow of virtue only, nor is there any freedom or health or truth in her; but in the true exchange there is a purging away of all these things, and temperance, and justice, and courage, and wisdom herself, are a purgation of them.

Comic

The comic and the tragic lie inseparably close, like light and shadow.

Command

What you cannot enforce, do not command.

Condemnation

Condemnation without investigation is the highest form of ignorance.

Confident

I am confident in the belief that there truly is such a thing as living again, and that the living spring from the dead, and that the souls of the dead are in existence, and that the good souls have a better portion than the evil.

I am confident that there truly is such a thing as living again, that the living spring from the dead, and that the souls of the dead are in existence.

Content

If all our misfortunes were laid in one common heap, whence everyone must take an equal portion, most people would be content to take their own and depart.

He who is not contented with what he has, would not be contented with what he would like to have.

Contentment

Contentment is natural wealth, luxury is artificial poverty.

Contentment is natural wealth.

Corrupt

Either I do not corrupt the young or, if I do, it is unwillingly.

Either I do not corrupt them, or I corrupt them unintentionally, so that on either view of the case you lie. If my offense is unintentional, the law has no cognizance of unintentional offenses; you ought to have taken me privately, and warned and admonished me; for if I had been better advised, I should have left off doing what I only did unintentionally — no doubt I should;

whereas you hated to converse with me or teach me, but you indicted me in this court, which is the place not of instruction, but of punishment.

Courage

Some have courage in pleasures, and some in pains: some in desires, and some in fears, and some are cowards under the same conditions.

Course

As to marriage or celibacy, let a man take which course he will-he will be sure to repent it.

Crito

Crito, I owe a cock to Asclepius; will you remember to pay the debt?

I would not have him sorrow at my hard lot, or say at the burial, Thus we lay out Socrates, or, Thus we follow him to the grave or bury him; for false words are not only evil in themselves, but they infect the soul with evil. Be of good cheer then, my good Crito, and say that you are burying my body only, and do with that as is usual, and as you think best.

Cure

Just as you ought not to attempt to cure eyes without head or head without body, so you should not treat body without soul.

The cure of many diseases remains unknown to the physicians of Hellos (Greece) because they do not study the whole person.

Danger

In every sort of danger there are various ways of winning through, if one is ready to do and say anything whatever.

Death

It is not difficult to avoid death, gentlemen of the jury; it is much more difficult to avoid wickedness, for it runs faster than death.

It is not difficult to avoid death. It is much more difficult to avoid wickedness, for it runs faster than death.

To fear death is nothing other than to think oneself wise when one is not. For it is to think one knows what one does not know. No one knows whether death may not even turn out to be the greatest blessings of human beings. And yet people fear it as if they knew for certain it is the greatest evil.

To fear death, gentlemen, is no other than to think oneself wise when one is not, to think one knows what one does not know. No one knows whether death may not be the greatest of all blessings for a man, yet men fear it as if they knew that it is the greatest of evils. And surely it is the most blameworthy ignorance to believe that one knows what one does not know. It is perhaps on this point and in this respect, gentlemen, that I differ from the majority of men, and if I were to claim that I am wiser than anyone in anything, it would be in this, that, as I have no adequate knowledge of things in the underworld, so I do not think I have. I do know, however, that it is wicked and shameful to do wrong, to disobey one's superior, be he god or man. I shall never fear or avoid things of which I do not know, whether they may not be good rather than things that I know to be bad.

To fear death, is nothing else but to believe ourselves to be wise, when we are not; and to fancy that we know what we do not know. In effect, nobody knows death; nobody can tell, but it may be the greatest benefit of mankind; and yet men are afraid of it, as if they knew certainly that it were the greatest of evils.

To fear death, my friends, is only to think ourselves wise, without being wise: for it is to think that we know what we do not know. For anything that men can tell, death may be the greatest good that can happen to them: but they fear it as if they knew quite well that it was the greatest of evils. And what is this but that shameful ignorance of thinking that we know what we do not know?

Be of good cheer about death, and know this of a truth, that no evil can happen to a good man, either in life or after death.

Be of good hope in the face of death. Believe in this one truth for certain, that no evil can befall a good man either in life or death, and that his fate is not a matter of indifference to the gods.

Death may be the greatest of all human blessings.

Death offers mankind a full view of truth.

If death had only been the end of all, the wicked would have had a good bargain in dying, for they would have been happily quit not only of their body, but of their own evil together with their souls. But now, as the soul plainly appears to be immortal, there is no release or salvation from evil except the attainment of the highest virtue and wisdom. For the soul when on her progress to the world below takes nothing with her but nurture and education.

Debate

When the debate is over, slander becomes the tool of the loser.

Deserve

Giving to the undeserving is the same as withholding from the deserving.

Desire

In every one of us there are two ruling and directing principles, whose guidance we follow wherever they may lead; the one being an innate desire of pleasure; the other, an acquired judgment which aspires after excellence.

Since all of us desire to be happy, and since we evidently become so on account of our use—that is our good use—of other things, and since knowledge is what provides this goodness of use and also good fortune, every man must, as seems plausible, prepare himself by every means for this: to be as wise as possible. Right?

From the deepest desires often come the deadliest hate.

Discord

If he who does not know kept silent, discord would cease.

Divine

I hold that to need nothing is divine, and the less a man needs the nearer does he approach divinity.

My divine sign indicates the future to me.

You think that upon the score of fore-knowledge and divining I am infinitely inferior to the swans. When they perceive approaching death they sing more merrily than before, because of the joy they have in going to the God they serve.

You will know that the divine is so great and of such a nature that it sees and hears everything at once, is present everywhere, and is concerned with everything.

Earth

If somebody asks them, Why, what evil does he practice or teach? They do not know, and cannot tell; but in order that they do not appear to be at a loss, they repeat the ready-made charges which are used against all philosophers about teaching things up in the clouds and under the earth, and having no gods, and making the worse appear the better cause; for they do not like to confess that their preteens of knowledge has been detected — which is the truth.

Education

An education obtained with money is worse than no education at all.

Education and seeing what one has not seen before.

Education is the kindling of a flame, not the filling of a vessel.

Effect

I do not know what effect my accusers have had upon you, gentlemen, but for my own part I was almost carried away by them; their arguments were so convincing. On the other hand, scarcely a word of what they said was true. But of the many falsehoods told by them, there was one which quite amazed me; I mean when they said that you should be upon your guard and not allow yourselves to be deceived by the force of my eloquence-the implication being that I am a skilful speaker. To say this, when they were certain to be detected as soon as I opened my lips and proved myself to be anything but a great speaker, did indeed appear to me most shameless—unless by the force of eloquence they mean the force of truth; for is such is their meaning, I admit that I am eloquent. But in how different away from theirs.

Employ

Employ your time in improving yourself by other men's writings so that you shall come easily by what others have laboured hard for.

Employ your time in improving yourself by other men's writings, so that you shall gain easily what others have laboured hard for.

Enjoy

Enjoy yourself it's later than you think.

Equal

Once made equal to man, woman becomes his superior.

Evil

There is but one evil, ignorance.

Exchange

The exchange of one fear or pleasure or pain for another fear or pleasure or pain, which are measured like coins, the greater with the less, is not the exchange of virtue. O, my dear Simmias, is there not one true coin, for which all things ought to exchange?—and that is wisdom; and only in exchange for this, and in company with this, is anything truly bought or sold, whether courage or temperance or justice. In the true exchange, there is a purging away of all these things, and temperance, and justice, and courage, and wisdom herself are a purgation of them.

Exercise

Exercise till the mind feels delight in reposing from the fatigue.

Express

To express oneself badly is not only faulty as far as the language goes, but does some harm to the soul.

Fact

We are in fact convinced that if we are ever to have pure knowledge of anything, we must get rid of the body and contemplate things by themselves with the soul by itself. It seems, to judge from the argument, that the wisdom which we desire and upon which we profess to have set our hearts will be attainable only when we are dead and not in our lifetime.

He knew nothing except just the fact of his ignorance.

Failure

Falling down is not a failure. Failure comes when you stay where you have fallen.

False

False language, evil in itself, infects the soul with evil.

False words are not only evil in themselves, but they infect the soul with evil.

Fame

Fame is the perfume of heroic deeds.

Fear

Fear of women love more than hate the man.

I shall never fear or avoid things of which I do not know.

Fellow

Fellow citizens, why do you burn and scrape every stone to gather wealth and take so little care of your children to whom you must one day relinquish all?

Find

To find the Father of all is hard. And when found, it is impossible to utter Him.

To find yourself, think for yourself.

Flattery

Flattery is like a painted armour; only for show.

Flattery is like friendship in show, but not in fruit.

Follow

Follow the argument wherever it leads.

Let us follow the truth whither so ever it leads.

Fool

I am a fool, but I know I'm a fool and that makes me smarter than you.

Friend

My friend, care for your psyche, know thyself, for once we know ourselves, we may learn how to care for ourselves.

The friend must be like money, that before you need it, the value is known.

Esteemed friend, citizen of Athens, the greatest city in the world, so outstanding in both intelligence and power, aren't you ashamed to care so much to make all the money you can, and to advance your reputation and prestige—while for truth and wisdom and the improvement of your soul you have no care or worry?

Get not your friends by bare compliments, but by giving them sensible tokens of your love.

The difficulty, my friends, is not in avoiding death, but in avoiding unrighteousness; for that runs faster than death.

Generation

If generation were in a straight line only, and there were no compensation or circle in nature, no turn or return into one another, then you know that all things would at last have the same form and pass into the same state, and there would be no more generation of them.

Genius

For after death, as they say, the genius of each individual, to whom he belonged in life, leads him to a certain place in which the dead are gathered together for judgment, whence they go into the world below, following the guide who is appointed to conduct them from this world to the other; and when they have there received their due and remained their time, another guide brings them back again after many revolutions of ages.

Give

They give you the semblance of success, I give you the reality.

Glory

The nearest way to glory a shortcut, as it were is to strive to be what you wish to be thought to be.

The nearest way to glory is to strive to be what you wish to be thought to be.

Go

Go wherever the facts lead.

God

God does not deal directly with man: it is by means of spirits that all the intercourse and communication of gods with men, both in waking life and in sleep, is carried on.

God takes away the minds of poets, and uses them as his ministers, as he also uses diviners and holy prophets, in order that we who hear them may know them to be speaking not of themselves who utter these priceless words in a state of unconsciousness, but that God himself is the speaker, and that through them he is conversing with us.

God would seem to indicate to us and not allow us to doubt that these beautiful poems are not human, or the work of man, but divine and the work of God; and that the poets are only the interpreters of the Gods.

I am quite ready to acknowledge that I ought to be grieved at death, if I were not persuaded that I am going to other gods who are wise and good (of this I am as certain as I can be of any such matters), and to men departed who are better than those whom I leave behind. And therefore I do not grieve as I might have done, for I have good hope that there is yet something remaining for the dead.

I am that gadfly which God has attached to the state, and all day long and in all places am always fastening upon you, arousing and persuading and reproaching you.

I have lived long enough to learn how much there is I can really do without. He is nearest to God who needs the fewest things.

I pray Thee, O God, that I may be beautiful within.

If I tell you that I would be disobeying the god and on that account it is impossible for me to keep quiet, you won't be persuaded by me, taking it that I am ionizing. And if I tell you that it is the greatest good for a human being to have discussions every day about virtue and the other things you hear me talking about, examining myself and others, and that the unexamined life is not liveable for a human being, you will be even less persuaded.

Is something good because the gods approve of it? Or do the gods approve of it because it is good?

It seems that God took away the minds of poets that they might better express Him.

The end of life is to be like God, and the soul following God will be like Him.

The end of life is to be like unto God; and the soul following God, will be like unto Him; He being the beginning, middle, and end of all things.

To give either to any public matter of interest or to any concern of my own, but I am in utter poverty by reason of my devotion to the god.

What do you say about making a libation out of this cup to any god? I may and I must pray to the gods to prosper my journey from this to that other world—may this, then, which is my prayer, be granted to me. (Then holding the cup to his lips, quite readily and cheerfully he drank off the poison. And hitherto most of us had been able to control their sorrow; but now, when we saw him drinking, and saw too, that he had finished the draft, we could no longer forbear, and in spite of myself my own tears were flowing fast; so that I covered my face and wept over myself, for certainly I was not weeping over him, but at my own calamity at having lost such a companion. Nor was I the first, for Crito, when he found himself unable to restrain his tears, had got up, and moved away, and I followed; and at that moment, Apollodorus, who had been weeping all the time, broke out in a loud cry which made cowards of us all. Socrates alone retained his calmness:) What is this strange outcry? I sent away the women mainly in order that they might not offend in this way, for I have heard that a man should die in peace. Be quiet then, and have patience.

And now we go, you to your lives, and I to death, and which of us goes to the better only God knows.

But already it is time to depart, for me to die, for you to go on living; which of us takes the better course, is concealed from anyone except God.

O beloved Pan and all ye other gods of this place, grant to me that I be made beautiful in my soul within, and that all external possessions be in harmony with my inner man. May I consider the wise man rich; and may I have such wealth as only the self-restrained man can bear or endure.

One cannot come closer to the gods than by bringing health to his Fellow Man.

The fewer our wants the more we resemble the Gods.

The poets are only the interpreters of the Gods.

Good

There is one way, then, in which a man can be free from all anxiety about the fate of his soul - if in life he has abandoned bodily pleasures and adornments, as foreign to his purpose and likely to do more harm than good, and has devoted himself to the pleasures of acquiring knowledge, and so by decking his soul not with a borrowed beauty but with its own - with self-control, and goodness, and courage, and liberality, and truth - has fitted himself to await his journey in the next world.

There is only one good, knowledge, and one evil, ignorance.

There's no good answer to a question you didn't hear.

To gain a good reputation, endeavour to be what you desire to appear.

Well, although I do not suppose that either of us know anything really beautiful and good, I am better off than he is- for he knows nothing & thinks that he knows; I neither know nor think that I know.

Would that the majority could inflict the greatest evils, for they would then be capable of the greatest good, and that would be fine, but now they cannot do either. They cannot make a man either wise or foolish, but they inflict things haphazardly.

You are not only good to yourself, but the cause of goodness in others.

Get married, in any case. If you happen to get a good mate, you will be happy; if a bad one, you will become philosophical, which is a fine thing in itself.

He said that there was one only good, namely, knowledge; and one only evil, namely, ignorance.

I did not go where I could do no good to you or to myself; but where I could do the greatest good privately to everyone of you, thither I went, and sought to persuade every man among you that he must look to himself, and seek virtue and wisdom before he looks to his private interests, and look to the State before he looks to the interests of the State; and that this should be the order which he observes in all his actions. What shall be done to such a one? Doubtless some good thing.

I prefer to be refuted than to refute, for it is a greater good for oneself to be freed from the greatest evil than to free another.

If what you want to tell me is neither True nor Good nor even Useful, why tell it to me at all.

In all of us, even in good men, there is a lawless wild-beast nature, which peers out in sleep.

It is the greatest good for an individual to discuss virtue every day for the unexamined life is not worth living.

The only good is knowledge and the only evil is ignorance.

Great

There are a great many of these accusers, and they have been accusing me now for a great many years, and what is more, they approached you at the most impressionable age, when some of you were children or adolescents; and literally won their case by default, because there was no one to defend me.

There is no greater evil one can suffer than to hate reasonable discourse.

There is no greater magnificence than to defeat oneself. That is the magnificence.

Is there anyone to whom you entrust a greater number of serious matters than your wife? And is there anyone with whom you have fewer conversations?

No one knows whether death may not be the greatest of all blessings for a man, yet men fear it as if they knew it was the greatest of evils.

Not that this confusion signifies to them who never care to think about the matter at all, for they have the wit to be well pleased with themselves, however great the turmoil of their ideas. But you, if you are a philosopher, will, I believe, do as I say.

Nothing is more uncommon than a very large or a very small man; and this applies generally to all extremes, whether of great and small, or swift and slow, or fair and foul, or black and white; and whether the instances you select be man or dogs or anything else, few are the extremes, but many are in the mean between them.

The greater the power that deigns to serve you, the more honour it demands of you.

The greatest blessing granted to mankind come by way of madness, which is a divine gift.

The greatest flood has the soonest ebb; the sorest tempest the most sudden calm; the hottest love the coldest end; and from the deepest desire oftentimes ensues the deadliest hate.

The greatest of all mysteries is the man himself.

Grow

It is a disgrace to grow old through sheer carelessness before seeing what manner of man you may become by developing your bodily strength and beauty to their highest limit.

When my sons are grown up, I would ask you, O my friends, to punish them; and I would have you to trouble them, as I have troubled you, if they seem to care about riches, or anything, more than about virtue; or if they pretend to be something when they are really nothing — then reprove them, as I have reproved you, for not caring about that for which they ought to care, and thinking that they are something when they are really nothing. And if you do this, I and my sons will have received justice at your hands.

Guide

If you will be guided by me, you will make little account of Socrates, and much more of truth.

Habit

We are what we repeatedly do. Excellence, then, is a habit.

Happiness

Happiness is unrepentant pleasure.

Happy

Happy indeed would be the condition of youth if they had one corrupter only, and all the rest of the world were their improvers.

Harm

To harm another is to harm oneself.

Harmony

It would be better for me that multitudes of men should disagree with me rather than that I, being one, should be out of harmony with myself.

Health

If you would seek health, look first to the spine.

Heart

Do it because it's in your heart. Not because you want something in return. Employ your time in improving yourself by other men's writings, so that you shall gain easily what others have laboured hard for.

Hope

I have good hope that there is something remaining for the dead.

I have had no regular disciples: but if anyone likes to come and hear me while I am pursuing my mission, whether he be young or old, he may freely come. Nor do I converse with those who pay only, and not with those who do not pay; but anyone, whether he be rich or poor, may ask and answer me and listen to my words; and whether he turns out to be a bad man or a good one, that cannot be justly laid to my charge, as I never taught him anything. And if anyone says that he has ever learned or heard anything from me in private which all the world has not heard, I should like you to know that he is speaking an untruth.

Hour

Now the hour to part has come. I go to die, you go to live. Which of us goes to the better lot is known to no one, except the god.

The hour of departure has arrived and we go our ways; I to die, and you to live. Which is better? Only God knows.

The hour of departure has arrived, and we go our separate ways, I to die, and you to live. Which of these two is better only God knows.

Hurt

When our feet hurt, we hurt all over.

Husband

A husband is what's left of the lover after the nerve has been extracted.

Idle

He is not only idle who does nothing, but he is idle who might be better employed.

They are not only idle who do nothing, but they are idle also who might be better employed.

Improve

Improve yourself by other men's writings thus attaining effortlessly what they acquired through great difficulty.

Incredible

It was far too cold. The second I got out I had this incredible headache, I'm just not used to it. The last time I saw snow was years and years ago.

Individual

The individual leads in order that those who are led can develop their potential as human beings and thereby prosper.

Each individual can only do one thing well. He can't do lots of things. If he tries, he will be jack of all trades, and master of none.

Information

The information, although eclectic as it spans from different cultures and time periods, interestingly ties together in several respects and it is this synchronicity that makes the information all the more remarkable.

Injure

It has been shown that to injure anyone is never just anywhere.

Injury

One who is injured ought not to return the injury, for on no account can it be right to do an injustice; and it is not right to return an injury, or to do evil to any man, however much we have suffered from him.

Ischomachus

Really, Ischomachus, I am disposed to ask: Does teaching consist in putting questions? Indeed, the secret of your system has just this instant dawned upon me. I seem to see the principle in which you put your questions. You lead me through the field of my own knowledge, and then by pointing out analogies to what I know, persuade me that I really know some things which hitherto, as I believed, I had no knowledge of.

Judge

Four things belong to a judge: to hear courteously, to answer wisely, to consider soberly, and to decide impartially.

Justice

Nothing is to be preferred before justice.

So you would rather suffer an injustice than do an injustice?

One ought not to return injustice, nor do evil to anybody in the world, no matter what one may have suffered from them.

Key

The tongue of a fool is the key of his counsel, which, in a wise man, wisdom hath in keeping.

Kicks

Why should I resent it when an ass kicks me?

Kind

Be kind, for everyone you meet is fighting a hard battle.

Know

I don't know why I did it, I don't know why I enjoyed it, and I don't know why i'll do it again.

I know I am intelligent, because I know that I know nothing.

I know nothing but the certainty of my own ignorance.

I know nothing except the fact of my ignorance.

I know that I know nothing.

To know thyself is the beginning of wisdom.

To know, is to know that you know nothing. That is the meaning of true knowledge.

To know, is to know that you know nothing. That is the meaning of true knowledge. For a man who claims to have knowledge, while actually knowing nothing, is less smarter than you, who claim to know nothing.

What I do not know, I do not think I know.

You don't know what you don't know.

All I know is that I do not know anything.

All that I know is nothing, I'm not even sure of that.

All that we know is nothing can be known.

And in knowing that you know nothing, that makes you the smartest of all.

As for me, all I know is that I know nothing, for when I don't know what justice is, i'll hardly know whether it is a kind of virtue or not, or whether a person who has it is happy or unhappy.

As for me, all I know is that I know nothing.

He who knows not and knows not that he knows not is an incorrigible fool.

Knowing thyself is the height of wisdom.

Nobody knows anything, but I, knowing nothing, am the smartest man in the world.

Nobody knows what death is Knowledge

Only the knowledge that comes from inside is the real Knowledge.

The only true knowledge, consists in knowing, that we know nothing.

Prefer knowledge to wealth, for the one is transitory, the other perpetual.

There is no difference between knowledge and temperance; for he who knows what is good and embraces it, who knows what is bad and avoids it, is learned and temperate.

This is self knowledge for a man to know what he knows, and what he does not know.

I soon realized that poets do not compose their poems with knowledge, but by some inborn talent and by inspiration, like seers and prophets who also say many fine things without any understanding of what they say.

If the knowledge which we acquired before birth was lost to us at birth, and afterwards by the use of the senses we recovered that which we previously knew, will not that which we call learning be a process of recovering our knowledge, and may not this be rightly termed recollection by us.

Language

The misuse of language induces evil in the soul.

Law

The law presumably says that it is finest to keep as quiet as possible in misfortunes and not be irritated, since the good and bad in such things aren't plain, nor does taking it hard get one anywhere, not are any of the human things worthy of great seriousness. One must accept the fall of the dice and settle one's affairs accordingly in whatever way argument declares would be best. One must not behave like children who have stumbled and who hold on to the hurt place and spend their time in crying out; rather one must always habituate the soul to turn as quickly as possible to curing and setting aright what has fallen and is sick, doing away with lament by medicine.

Learn

Nothing is so well learned as that which is discovered.

Learning

There is no learning without remembering.

Life

What screws us up the most in life is the picture in our head of what it's supposed to be.

Wherefore, O judges, be of good cheer about death, and know that this is of a truth—that no evil can happen to a good man, either in life or after death. For which reason also, I am not angry with my accusers, or my condemners; they have done me no harm, although neither of them meant to do me any good; and for this I may gently blame them.

A Life without criticism and status is not a worth living.

An unconsidered life is not one worth living.

An unexamined life is not worth living.

Beware the barrenness of a busy life.

Do not go through life like leaf blown from here to there believing whatever you are told.

Don't be embarrassed to become better at the end of your life than you were when you begun.

I have not sought during my life to amass wealth and to adorn my body, but I have sought to adorn my soul with the jewels of wisdom, patience, and above all with a love of liberty.

If my life is to be prolonged now, I know that I must live out my old age, seeing worse, hearing less, learning with more difficulty, and forgetting more and more of what I have learned. If I see myself growing worse and reproach myself for it, tell me, how could I continue to live pleasantly? Perhaps even the god in his kindness is offering to end my life not only at the right time, but also in the easiest way possible.

In the course of my life I have often had intimations in dreams "that I should make music." The same dream came to me sometimes in one form, and sometimes in another, but always saying the same or nearly the same words: Make and cultivate music, said the dream. And hitherto I imagined that this was only intended to exhort and encourage me in the study of philosophy, which has always been the pursuit of my life, and is the noblest and best of music.

In this present life, I reckon that we make the nearest approach to knowledge when we have the least possible concern or interest in the body, and are not saturated with the bodily nature, but remain pure until the hour when God himself is pleased to release us. And then the foolishness of the body will be cleared away and we shall be pure and hold converse with other pure souls, and know of ourselves the clear light everywhere; and this is surely the light of truth. For no impure thing is allowed to approach the pure. These are the sort of words, Simmias, which the true lovers of wisdom cannot help saying to one another, and thinking.

It is only in death that we are truly cured of the 'sickness' of life.

Life contains but two tragedies. One is not to get your heart's desire; the other is to get it.

Life without enquiry is not worth living for a man.

Life without enquiry is not worth living.

Marry a good woman, and be happy the rest of your life. Or, marry a bad, and become a good philosopher.

Not life, but good life, is to be chiefly valued.

Not life, but good life, is to be chiefly valued. It is not living that matters, but living rightly. The unexamined life is not worth living.

So long as I have life and strength I shall never cease from the practice and teaching of philosophy, exhorting you and elucidating the truth for everyone that I meet. I shall go on saying, in my usual way, My friend, you are an Athenian and belong to a city which is the greatest and famous in the world for its wisdom and strength. Are you not ashamed that you give your attention to acquiring as much money as possible, and similarly with honour and reputation, and care so little about wisdom and truth and the greatest improvement of the soul, which you never regard or heed at all?

Such as thy words are such will thine affections be esteemed and such as thine affections will be thy deeds and such as thy deeds will be thy life.

Such as thy words are, such will thy affections be esteemed; and such will thy deeds be as thy affections and such thy life as thy deeds.

The examined life is the only life worth living.

The I unexamined life is not worth living.

The life of which meaning one never ponders is not worth living.

The life which is unexamined is not worth living.

The real danger in life is not death, but living an evil life.

Line

You never know a line is crooked unless you have a straight one to put next to it.

Listen

Listen not to a tale-bearer or slanderer, for he tells thee nothing out of good-will; but as he discovered of the secrets of others, so he will of thine in turn.

Little

I myself know nothing, except just a little, enough to extract an argument from another man who is wise and to receive it fairly.

I only know how little I know.

If you can do only a little. Do what you can. What you cannot enforce, do not command. He who is not contented with what he has, would not be contented with what he would like to have.

If you can do only a little. Do what you can. What you cannot enforce, do not command.

Live

Most people, including ourselves, live in a world of relative ignorance. We are even comfortable with that ignorance, because it is all we know. When we first start facing truth, the process may be frightening, and many people run back to their old lives. But if you continue to seek truth, you will eventually be able to handle it better. In fact, you want more! It's true that many people around you now may think you are weird or even a danger to society, but you don't care. Once you've tasted the truth, you won't ever want to go back to being ignorant.

The greatest way to live with honour in this world is to be what we pretend to be.

The greatest way to live with honour in this world is to be what we pretend to be; and if we observe, we shall find, that all human virtues increase and strengthen themselves by the practice of them.

The greatest way to live with honour in this world is to be what we pretend to be.

The really important thing is not live, but to live well.

The really important thing is not to live, but to live well. And to live well meant, along with more enjoyable things in life, to live according to your principles.

The shortest and surest way to live with honour in the world is to be in reality what we would appear to be; and if we observe, we shall find that all human virtues increase and strengthen themselves by the practice and experience of them.

To live well and honourably and justly are the same thing.

We cannot live better than in seeking to become better.

Those also who are remarkable for having led holy lives are released from this earthly prison, and go to their pure home which is above, and dwell in the purer earth; and those who have duly purified themselves with philosophy live henceforth altogether without the body, in mansions fairer far than these.

Thus such another will not easily come to you, men, but if you believe me, you will spare me; but perhaps you might possibly be offended, like the sleeping who are awakened, striking me, believing Anytus, you might easily kill, then the rest of your lives you might continue sleeping, unless the god caring for you should send you another.

What most counts is not merely to live, but to live right.

You should eat to live; not live to eat.

If I am to live longer, perhaps I must live out my old age, seeing and hearing less, understanding worse, coming to learn with more difficulty and to be more forgetful, and growing worse than those to whom I was once superior. Indeed, life would be unliveable, even if I did not notice the change. And if I see the change, how could life not be even more wretched and unpleasant?

Living or dead, to a good man there can come no evil.

Living well and beautifully and justly are all one thing.

Lives

Our lives are but specks of dust falling through the fingers of time. Like sands of the hourglass, so are the days of our lives.

Love

Two things greater than all the things are. On is love and the other is war.

Before the birth of Love, many fearful things took place through the empire of necessity; but when this god was born, all things rose to men.

I honour and love you: but why do you who are citizens of the great and mighty nation care so much about laying up the greatest amount of money and honour And reputation, and so little amount wisdom and truth and the greatest improvement of the soul? Re you not ashamed of these? I do nothing but go about persuading you all, not to take thought for your persons and your properties, but first and chiefly to care about the greatest improvement of the soul. I tell you that virtue is not given by more, but that from virtue comes money and every other good of man.

The hottest love has the coldest end.

I love to go and see all the things I am happy without.

In the acquisition of this blessing human nature can find no better helper than Love. I declare that it is the duty of every man to honour Love, and I honour and practice the mysteries of

Love in an especial degree myself, and recommend the same to others, and I praise the power and valour of Love to the best of my ability both now and always.

The warm love has the coldest end.

Those who are hardest to love need it the most.

Lover

And when you see a man who is repining at the approach of death, is not his reluctance a sufficient proof that he is not a lover of wisdom, but a lover of the body, and probably at the same time a lover of either money or power, or both?

And will he who is a true lover of wisdom, and is persuaded in like manner that only in the world below can he worthily enjoy her, still repine at death? Will he not depart with joy? Surely he will, my friend, if he be a true philosopher. And if this be true, he would be very absurd,...if he were to fear death.

Majority

Why should we pay so much attention to what the majority thinks?

Malice

Malice drink up the greater part of its own poison.

Man

Man must rise above the Earth - to the top of the atmosphere and beyond - for only thus will he fully understand the world in which he lives.

Mankind is made of two kinds of people: wise people who know they're fools, and fools who think they are wise.

Man's life is like a drop of dew on a leaf.

May I consider the wise man rich, and may I have such wealth as only the self-restrained man can bear or endure.

May the outward and inward man be at one.

The man who is truly wise knows that he knows very little.

Three sieves? The man asks What three sieves?

Well no, I just overheard it The man says.

What a lot of things there are a man can do without.

You are wrong, sir, if you think that a man who is any good at all should take into account the risk of life or death; he should look to this only in his actions, whether what he does is right or wrong, whether he is acting like a good or a bad man.

A good man cannot be harmed either in life or in death, and that his affairs are not neglected by the gods.

A good man cannot be harmed either in life or in death.

A man can no more make a safe use of wealth without reason than he can of a horse without a bridle.

A man should inure himself to voluntary labour, and not give up to indulgence and pleasure, as they beget no good constitution of body nor knowledge of mind.

A man who really fights for justice must lead a private, not a public, life if he is to survive for even a short time.

An envious man waxed lean with the fatness of his neighbours. Envy is the daughter of pride, the author of murder and revenge, the beginner of secret sedition and the perpetual tormentor of virtue. Envy is the filthy slime of the soul; a venom, a poison, or quicksilver which consumed the flesh and driest up the marrow of the bones.

An honest man is always a child.

Call no man unhappy until he is married.

He is a man of courage who does not run away, but remains at his post and fights against the enemy.

How can you call a man free when his pleasures rule over him.

I am the wisest man alive, for I know one thing, and that is that I know nothing.

I might fairly reply to him, 'You are mistaken, my friend, if you think that a man who is worth anything ought to spend his time weighing up the prospects of life and death. He has only one thing to consider in performing any action that is, whether he is acting rightly or wrongly, like a good man or a bad one.

I thought to myself, I am wiser than this man neither of us knows anything that is really worthwhile, but he thinks he has knowledge when he has not, while I, having no knowledge, do not think that I have. I seem, at any rate, to be a little wiser than he is on this point I do not think that I know what I do not know.

If a man comes to the door of poetry untouched by the madness of the Muses, believing that technique alone will make him a good poet, he and his sane compositions never reach perfection, but are utterly eclipsed by the performances of the inspired madman.

If any man could arrive at the exterior limit, or take the wings of a bird and fly upward, like a fish who puts his head out and sees the world, he would see a world beyond; and, if the nature of man could sustain this sight, he would acknowledge that this was the place of the true heaven and the true light and the true stars. For this earth, and the stones, and the entire region which surrounds us, are spoilt and corroded.

It is a base thing for a man to wax old in careless self-neglect before he has lifted up his eyes and seen what manner of man he was made to be, in the full perfection of bodily strength and beauty. But these glories are withheld from him who is guilty of self-neglect, for they are not wont to blaze forth unbidden.

It is possible that a man could live twice as long if he didn't spend the first half of his life acquiring habits that shortens the other half.

Neither I nor any other man should, on trial or in way, contrive to avoid death at any cost.

Neither in war nor yet at law ought any man to use every way of escaping death. For often in battle there is no doubt that if a man will throw away his arms, and fall on his knees before his pursuers, he may escape death; and in other dangers there are other ways of escaping death, if a man is willing to say and do anything. The difficulty, my friends, is not in avoiding death, but in avoiding unrighteousness; for that runs faster than death.

No man has the right to be an amateur in the matter of physical training. It is a shame for a man to grow old without seeing the beauty and strength of which his body is capable.

No man undertakes a trade he has not learned, even the meanest; yet everyone thinks himself sufficiently qualified for the hardest of all trades, that of government.

Manage

Whom do I call educated? First, those who manage well the circumstances they encounter day by day. Next, those who are decent and honourable in their intercourse with all men, bearing easily and good naturedly what is offensive in others and being as agreeable and reasonable to their associates as is humanly possible to be those who hold their pleasures always under control and are not ultimately overcome by their misfortunes those who are not spoiled by their successes, who do not desert their true selves but hold their ground steadfastly as wise and sober minded men.

Mankind

If all the misfortunes of mankind were cast into a public stack in order to be equally distributed among the whole species, those who now think themselves the most unhappy would prefer the share they are already possessed of before that which would fall to them by such a division.

Manner

It is not lack of arguments that has caused my condemnation; but I had not the boldness or impudence or inclination to address you as you would have liked me to do, weeping and wailing and lamenting, and saying and doing many things which you have been accustomed to hear from others, and which, as I maintain, are unworthy of me. I thought at the time that I ought not to do anything common or mean when in danger: nor do I now repent of the style of my defence; I would rather die having spoken after my manner, than speak in your manner and live.

I would rather die having spoken in my manner, than speak in your manner and live. For neither in war nor yet in law ought any man use every way of escaping death. For often in battle there is no doubt that if a man will throw away his arms, and fall on his knees before his pursuers, he may escape death, if a man is willing to say or do anything. The difficulty, my friends, is not in avoiding death, but in avoiding unrighteousness; for that runs deeper than death.

Marry

By all implies marry if you get a great wife/husband, you are going to be pleased. If you get a bad a single, you are going to become a philosopher.

By all means marry. If you get a good wife, you'll be happy. If you get a bad one, you'll become a philosopher and that is a good thing for any man.

Mathematics

The understanding of mathematics is necessary for a sound grasp of ethics.

Matter

It is not living that matters, but living rightly.

One should never do wrong in return, nor mistreat any man, no matter how one has been mistreated by him.

Measure

If measure and symmetry are absent from any composition in any degree, ruin awaits both the ingredients and the composition. Measure and symmetry are beauty and virtue the world over.

Meletus

I have said enough in answer to the charge of Meletus: any elaborate defense is unnecessary; but as I was saying before, I certainly have many enemies, and this is what will be my destruction if I am destroyed; of that I am certain; not Meletus, nor yet Anytus, but the envy and detraction of the world, which has been the death of many a good men, and will probably be the death of many more; there is no danger of my being the last of them.

Men

If thou continuous to take delight in idle argumentation thou may be qualified to combat with the sophists, but will never know how to live with men.

Bad men live that they may eat and drink, whereas good men eat and drink that they may live.

Base men live to eat and drink, and good men eat and drink to live.

For each of them, men, is able, going into each of the cities, to persuade the young-who can associate with whomever of their own citizens they wish to for free-they persuade these young men to leave off their associations with the latter, and to associate with themselves instead, and to give them money and acknowledge gratitude besides.

Mind

If mind is the disposer, mind will dispose all for the best, and put each particular in the best place; and I argued that if anyone desired to find out the cause of the generation or destruction of anything, he must find out what state of being or suffering or doing was best for that thing, and therefore a man had only consider the best for himself and others, and then he would also know the worse, for that the same science comprised both.

In order that the mind should see light instead of darkness, so the entire soul must be turned away from this changing world, until its eye can learn to contemplate reality and that supreme splendour which we have called the good. Hence there may well be an art whose aim would be to effect this very thing.

The mind is everything; what you think you become.

The mind is the pilot of the soul.

A multitude of books distracts the mind.

And now that the hour of departure is appointed to me, this is the hope with which I depart, and not I only, but every man that believes that he has his mind purified.

The invention of writing will produce forgetfulness in the minds of those who learn to use it, because they will not practice their memory. Their trust in writing, produced by external characters which are no part of themselves, will discourage the use of their own memory within them. You have invented an elixir not of memory, but of reminding; and you offer your pupils the appearance of wisdom, not true wisdom.

Mirror

The heart of the person before you is a mirror. See there your own form.

Money

Aren't you ashamed to be concerned so much about making all the money you can and advancing your reputation and prestige, while for truth and wisdom and the improvement of your souls you have no thought or car?

Money and honour have no attraction for them; good men do not wish to be openly demanding payment for governing and so to get the name of hirelings, nor by secretly helping themselves out of the public revenues to get the name of thieves. And not being ambitious they do not care about honour. Wherefore necessity must be laid upon them, and they must be induced to serve from the fear of punishment. And this, as I imagine, is the reason why the forwardness to take office, instead of waiting to be compelled, has been deemed dishonourable. Now the worst part of the punishment is that he who refuses to rule is liable to be ruled by one who is worse than himself. And the fear of this, as I conceive, induces the good to take office, not because they would, but because they cannot help — not under the idea that they are going to have any benefit or enjoyment themselves, but as a necessity, and because they are not able to commit the task of ruling to anyone who is better than themselves, or indeed as good. For there is reason to think that if a city were composed entirely of good men, then to avoid office would be as much an object of contention as to obtain office is at present.

More

The more I know, the more I realize that I know nothing.

The more I learn, the less I realize I know.

Move

To move the world we must move ourselves.

Let he who would move the world, first complete an environmental impact assessment and a 90-day public comment period.

Let him that would move the world, first move himself.

Music

Musical training is a more potent instrument than any other, because rhythm and harmony find their way into the inward places of the soul, on which they mightily fasten, imparting grace, and making the soul of him who is rightly educated graceful, or of him who is ill-educated ungraceful.

Mystery

There is a doctrine whispered in secret that a man is a prisoner who has no right to open the door and run away; this is a great mystery which I do not quite understand.

Mystery

I conceive that the founders of the mysteries had a real meaning and were not mere triflers when they intimated in a figure long ago that he who passes unsanctified and uninitiated into the world below will live in a slough, but that he who arrives there after initiation and purification will dwell with the gods. For "many," as they say in the mysteries, "are the thyrsus bearers, but few are the mystics,"—meaning, as I interpret the words, the true philosophers.

Nature

If you kill such a one as I am, you will injure yourselves more than you will injure me. Meletus and Anytus will not injure me: they cannot; for it is not in the nature of things that a bad man should injure one better than himself. I do not deny that he may, perhaps, kill him, or drive him into exile, or deprive him of civil rights; and he may imagine, and others may imagine, that he is doing him a great injury: but in that I do not agree with him; for the evil of doing what Anytus is doing — of unjustly taking away another man's life — is greater far.

Nature has given us two ears, two eyes, and but one tongue-to the end that we should hear and see more than we speak.

I am by nature filled with desire, for worldly pleasures, but I have mastered and subjugated myself.

Need

To need nothing is divine, and the less a man needs the nearer does he approach to divinity.

New

Nothing very new. By taking good care of yourselves you are of service to me and my family as well as yourselves, no matter what you do, even if you don't think so at present. But if you neglect yourselves and are unwilling to live, as though following tracks, in accordance with what we now say and have said in the past too, then no matter how much or how seriously you agree with me at present you will accomplish next to nothing.

Noble

The noblest worship is to make yourself as good and as just as you can.

Obligation

Obligation sends the children to bed on time, but love tucks the covers in around their necks and passes out kisses and hugs. Yesterday is about experience; tomorrow is about hope; today is about transitioning from one to the other. The happiest people on earth don't have the best of everything they make the best of everything I cannot teach anybody anything, I can only make them think.

Obscurity

Obscurity is dispelled by augmenting the light of discernment, not by attacking the darkness.

Oracle

The ancient Oracle said that I was the wisest of all the Greeks. It is because I alone, of all the Greeks, know that I know nothing.

The Delphic Oracle said that I was the wisest of all the Greeks. It is because I alone of all the Greeks know that I know nothing.

Ordinary

Ordinary people seem not to realize that those who really apply themselves in the right way to philosophy are directly and of their own accord preparing themselves for dying and death.

Pan

Beloved Pan and all ye other gods who haunt this place, give me beauty in the inward soul, and may the outward and the inner man be at one.

Oh dear Pan and all the other gods of this place, grant that I may be beautiful inside. Let all my external possessions be in friendly harmony with what is within. May I consider the wise man rich. As for gold, let me have as much as a moderate man could bear and carry with him.

Partisan

The partisan when he is engaged in a dispute, cares nothing about the rights of the question, but is anxious only to convince his hearers of his own assertions.

Path

If we pursue our habit of eating animals, and if our neighbour follows a similar path, will we need to go to war against our neighbour to secure greater pasturage, because ours will not be enough to sustain us, and our neighbour will have a similar need to wage war on us for the same reason.

People

I did not care for the things that most people care about– making money, having a comfortable home, high military or civil rank, and all the other activities, political appointments, secret societies, party organizations, which go on in our city. I set myself to do you– each one of you, individually and in private– what I hold to be the greatest possible service. I tried to persuade each one of you to concern himself less with what he has than with what he is, so as to render himself as excellent and as rational as possible.

I only wish that ordinary people had an unlimited capacity for doing harm; then they might have an unlimited power for doing good.

People demand freedom of speech to make up for the freedom of thought which they avoid.

People learn more on their own rather than being force fed.

Stupid people already have all the answers.

Whenever, therefore, people are deceived and form opinions wide of the truth, it is clear that the error has slid into their minds through the medium of certain resemblances to that truth.

Worthless people love only to eat and drink; people of worth eat and drink only to live.

Perfect

The perfect human being is all human beings put together, it is a collective, it is all of us together that make perfection.

Person

Be the kind of person that you want people to think you are.

In every person there is a sun. Just let them shine.

The envious person grows lean with the fatness of their neighbour.

Philebus

Philebus was saying that enjoyment and pleasure and delight, and the class of feelings akin to them, are a good to every living being, whereas I contend, that not these, but wisdom and intelligence and memory, and their kindred, right opinion and true reasoning, are better and more desirable than pleasure.

Philosopher

Has a philosopher like you failed to discover that our country is more to be valued and higher and holier far than mother or father or any ancestor, and more to be regarded in the eyes of the gods and of men of understanding?

He who has lived as a true philosopher has reason to be of good cheer when he is about to die, and that after death he may hope to receive the greatest good in the other world.

Philosophy

The philosophy exam was a piece of cake which was a bit of a surprise, actually, because I was expecting some questions on a sheet of paper.

Do not trouble about those who practice philosophy, whether they are good or bad; but examine the thing itself well and carefully. And if philosophy appears a bad thing to you, turn every man from it, not only your sons; but if it appears to you such as I think it to be, take courage, pursue it, and practice it, as the saying is, 'both you and your house.

Plain

Everything is plainer when spoken than when unspoken.

Pleasure

When the feeling of pleasure or pain in the soul is most intense, all of us naturally suppose that the object of this intense feeling is then plainest and truest; but this is not the case, because each pleasure and pain is a sort of nail which nails and rivets the soul to the body, and engrosses her and makes her believe that to be true which the body affirms to be true; and from agreeing with the body and having the same delights she is obliged to have the same habits and ways, and is not likely ever to be pure at her departure to the world below, but is always saturated with the body; so that she soon (after death) sinks into another body and there germinates and grows, and has therefore no part in the communion of the divine and pure and simple.

Every pleasure or pain has a sort of rivet with which it fastens the soul to the body and pins it down and makes it corporeal, accepting as true whatever the body certifies.

Poet

For the poet is a light and winged and holy thing, and there is no invention in him until he has been inspired and is out of his senses, and the mind is no longer in him: when he has not attained to this state, he is powerless and is unable to utter his oracles.

From poets, I moved to artists. No one was more ignorant about the arts than I; no one was more convinced that artists possessed really beautiful secrets. However, I noticed that their condition was no better than that of the poets and that both of them have the same misconceptions. Because the most skilful among them excel in their specialty, they look upon themselves as the wisest of men. In my eyes, this presumption completely tarnished their knowledge. As a result, putting myself in the place of the oracle and asking myself what I would prefer to be—what I was or what they were, to know what they have learned or to know that I know nothing—I replied to myself and to the god: I wish to remain who I am.

I examined the poets, and I look on them as people whose talent overawes both themselves and others, people who present themselves as wise men and are taken as such, when they are nothing of the sort.

Politician

I was really too honest a man to be a politician and live.

Politics

If I had engaged in politics, I should have perished long ago and done no good to either you or to myself. For the truth is that no man who goes to war with you or any other multitude, honestly struggling against the commission of unrighteousness and wrong in the State, will save his life; he who will really fight for right, if he would live even for a little while, must have a private station and not a public one.

Position

I have examined your position and determined your utterances to be mere brain-farts. But even so, supposing you should try to think afresh, your thoughts will be better as a consequence of today's scrutiny.

Possession

There is no possession more valuable than a good and faithful friend.

Power

For who is there but you? Who not only claim to be a good man and a gentleman, for many are this, and yet have not the power of making others good. Whereas you are not only good yourself, but also the cause of goodness in others.

Practice

Serenity, regularity, absence of vanity, sincerity, simplicity, veracity, equanimity, fixity, non-irritability, adaptability, humility, tenacity, integrity, nobility, magnanimity, charity, generosity, purity. Practise daily these eighteen ities, You will soon attain immortality.

Praise

Think not those faithful who praise all thy words and actions; but those who kindly reprove thy faults.

Prayers

Our prayers should be for blessings in general, for God knows best what is good for us.

Pride

Pride divides the men, humility joins them.

Principle

You would say inexperienced as I am, and ready to start, as the proverb says, at my own shadow, I cannot afford to give up the sure ground of principle and when you are further required to give an explanation of this principle, you would go on to assume a higher principle, and the best of the higher ones, until you found a resting place; but you would not refuse the principle and consequences in your reasoning like the Eristics—at least if you wanted to discover real existence.

Programming

Programming is not about what you know.

Proud

If a rich man is proud of his wealth, he should not be praised until it is known how he employs it.

Purpose

It is not the purpose of a juryman's office to give justice as a favour to whoever seems good to him, but to judge according to law, and this he has sworn to do.

Our purpose in founding the city was not to make any one class in it surpassingly happy, but to make the city as a whole as happy as possible.

Reason

The reason why we have to acquire wealth is the body, because we are slaves in its service.

When desire, having rejected reason and overpowered judgment which leads to right, is set in the direction of the pleasure which beauty can inspire, and when again under the influence of its kindred desires it is moved with violent motion towards the beauty of corporeal forms, it acquires a surname from this very violent motion, and is called love.

Reflect

Let us reflect in this way, too, that there is good hope that death is a blessing, for it is one of two things: either the dead are nothing and have no perception of anything, or it is, as we are told, a change and a relocation for the soul from here to another place.

Regard

Regard your good name as the richest jewel you can possibly be possessed of — for credit is like fire; when once you have kindled it you may easily preserve it, but if you once extinguish it, you will find it an arduous task to rekindle it again. The way to a good reputation is to endeavour to be what you desire to appear.

Remember

Remember that there is nothing stable in human affairs; therefore avoid undue elation in prosperity, or undue depression in adversity.

Remember what is unbecoming to do is also unbecoming to speak of.

Remember, no human condition is ever permanent. Then you will not be overjoyed in good fortune nor too scornful in misfortune.

Reverence

Where there is reverence there is fear, but there is not reverence everywhere that there is fear, because fear presumably has a wider extension than reverence.

Rich

He is richest who is content with the least, for content is the wealth of nature.

He is the richest who is content with the least.

Right

When you belong to a minority, you have to be better in order to have the right to be equal.

If one knows what is right, he will do it; nobody wants to be evil.

Sale

Often when looking at a mass of things for sale, he would say to himself, 'How many things I have no need of!'

School

I found this book to be a very interesting gathering of information and collection of obscure and/or remote antiquated information, i.e. Biblical, sacred, mythological and otherwise, that we were not exactly taught to us in bible school, or any other public school for that matter. And I am of the school of thought that has been so for intended purposes.

Science

Science says, We must live and seeks the means of prolonging, increasing, facilitating and amplifying life, of making it tolerable and acceptable, wisdom says, We must die and seeks how to make us die well.

Secret

The secret of change is to focus all of your energy, not on fighting the old, but on building the new.

The secret of change is to focus all your energy, not fighting the old, but on building the new.

The secret of happiness, you see, is not found in seeking more, but in developing the capacity to enjoy less.

See

See one promontory, one mountain, one sea, one river and see all.

Self

Be true to the own self.

I must first know myself, as the Delphi an inscription says; to be curious about that which is not my concern, while I am still in ignorance of my own self, would be ridiculous. And therefore

I bid farewell to all this; the common opinion is enough for me. For, as I was saying, I want to know not about this, but about myself: am I a monster more complicated and swollen with passion than the serpent Typhoo, or a creature of a gentler and simpler sort, to whom Nature has given a diviner and lowlier destiny?

Service

In my investigation in the service of the god I found that those who had the highest reputation were nearly the most deficient, while those who were thought to be inferior were more knowledgeable.

Sieve

Ah, well then you have used the second sieve, the sieve of good? Socrates asks Is it something good what you're about to tell me?

Silence

Silence is a profound melody, for those who can hear it above all the noise.

Silent

I wish that those who do not know would simply remain silent.

Skill

When a simple man who has no skill in dialectics believes an argument to be true which he afterwards imagines to be false, whether really false or not, and then another and another, he no longer has any faith left, and great disputers, as you know, come to think, at last that they have grown to be the wisest of mankind; for they alone perceive the utter unsoundness and instability of all arguments, or, indeed, of all things, which like the currents in the Euripus, are going up and down in never-ceasing ebb and flow.

Slanderer

Slanderers do not hurt me because they do not hit me.

Smart

Smart people learn from everything and everyone.

Society

He who is unable to live in society, or who has no need because he is sufficient for himself, must be either a beast or a god.

Socrates

Socrates, of a course of life which is likely to bring you to an untimely end? To him I may fairly answer: There you are mistaken: a man who is good for anything ought not to calculate the chance of living or dying; he ought only to consider whether in doing anything he is doing right or wrong — acting the part of a good man or a bad....For wherever a man's place is, whether the place he has chosen or that where he has been placed by a commander. There he ought to remain in the hour of danger; he should not think of death or of anything, but of disgrace.

Someone will say: Yes, Socrates, but cannot you hold your tongue, and then you may go into a foreign city, and no one will interfere with you? Now I have great difficulty in making you understand my answer to this. For if I tell you that this would be a disobedience to a divine command, and therefore that I cannot hold my tongue, you will not believe that I am serious; and if I say that the greatest good of a man is daily to converse about virtue, and all that concerning which you hear me examining myself and others, and that the life which is unexamined is not worth living — that you are still less likely to believe.

Solution

There is no solution; seek it lovingly.

Soul

You want to have proven to you that the soul is imperishable and immortal, and you think that the philosopher who is confident in death has but a vain and foolish confidence, if he thinks that he will fare better than one who has led another sort of life, in the world below, unless he can prove this; and you say that the strength and divinity of the soul, and of her existence prior to our becoming men, does not necessarily imply her immortality.... For any man, who is not devoid of natural feeling, has reason to fear, if he has no knowledge or proof of the soul's immortality. That is what I suppose you to say, Cebes, which I designedly repeat, in order that nothing may escape us.

A free soul ought not to pursue any study slavishly, for nothing that is learned under compulsion stays with the mind.

And the same things look bent and straight when seen in water and out of it, and also both concave and convex, due to the sight's being mislead by the colours, and every sort of confusion of this kind is plainly in our soul. And, then, it is because they take advantage of this affection in our nature that shadow painting, and puppeteering, and many other tricks of the kind fall nothing short of wizardry.

And therefore if the head and the body are to be well, you must begin by curing the soul; that is the first and essential thing. And the care of the soul, my dear youth, has to be effected by the use of certain charms, and these charms are fair words; and by them temperance is implanted in the soul, and where temperance comes and stays, there health is speedily imparted, not only to the head, but to the whole body.

But the soul which has been polluted, and is impure at the time of her departure, and is the companion and servant of the body always, and is in love with and fascinated by the body and by the desires and pleasures of the body, until she is led to believe that the truth exists only in bodily form, which a man may touch and see and taste and use for the purposes of his lusts—the soul, I mean, accustomed to hate and fear and avoid the intellectual principle, which to the bodily eye is dark and invisible, and can be attained only by philosophy—do you suppose that such a soul as this will depart pure and unalloyed?

But when returning into herself she [the soul] reflects; then she passes into the realm of purity, and eternity, and immortality, and unchangeableness, which are her kindred, and with them she ever lives, when she is by herself and is not let or hindered; then she ceases from her erring ways, and being in communion with the unchanging is unchanging. And this state of the soul is called wisdom.

Envy is the ulcer of the soul.

I do not mean to affirm that the description which I have given of the soul and her missions is exactly true—a man of sense ought hardly say that. But I do say that, inasmuch as the soul is shown to be immortal, he may venture to think, not improperly or unworthily, that something of this kind is true.

I shall never cease from the practice and teaching of philosophy, exhorting anyone whom I meet after my manner, and convincing him, saying: O my friend, why do you who are a citizen of the great and mighty and wise city of Athens, care so much about laying up the greatest amount of money and honour and reputation, and so little about wisdom and truth and the greatest improvement of the soul, which you never regard or heed at all? Are you not ashamed of this? And if the person with whom I am arguing says: Yes, but I do care: I do not depart or let him go at once; I interrogate and examine and cross-examine him, and if I think that he has no virtue, but only says that he has, I reproach him with overvaluing the greater, and undervaluing the less. For this is the command of God, as I would have you know.

I shall never cease from the practice and teaching of philosophy, exhorting anyone whom I meet after my manner, and convincing him, saying: O my friend, why do you who are a citizen of the great and mighty and wise city of Athens, care so much about laying up the greatest amount of money and honour and reputation, and so little about wisdom and truth and the greatest improvement of the soul, which you never regard or heed at all? Are you not ashamed of this?

I thought that as I had failed in the contemplation of true existence, I ought to be careful that I did not lose the eye of my soul; as people may injure their bodily eye by observing and gazing on the sun during an eclipse, unless they take the precaution of looking at the image reflected in the water, or in some similar medium. I was afraid that my soul might be blinded altogether if I looked at things with my eyes or tried by the help of my senses to apprehend them. And I thought that I had better had recourse to ideas, and seek in them truth in existence. I dare to say that the simile is not perfect—for I am far from admitting that he who contemplates existence through the medium of ideas, sees them only through a glass darkly, any more than he who sees them in their working and effects.

I was afraid that by observing objects with my eyes and trying to comprehend them with each of my other senses I might blind my soul altogether.

If the immortal is also imperishable, the soul when attacked by death cannot perish; for the preceding argument shows that the soul will not admit of death, or even be dead, any more than three or the odd number will admit of the event.

If the soul is immortal, it demands our care not only for that part of time which we call life, but for all time: and indeed it would seem now that it will be extremely dangerous to neglect it. If death were a release from everything, it would be a boon for the wicked. But since the soul is clearly immortal, it can have no escape or security from evil except by becoming as good and wise as it possibly can. For it takes nothing with it to the next world except its education and training: and these, we are told, are of supreme importance in helping or harming the newly dead at the very beginning of his journey there.

Suppose that there are two sorts of existences, one seen, and the other unseen. The scene is the changing, and the unseen is the unchanging.. And further, is not one part of us body, and the rest of us soul? Then the soul is more like to the unseen, and the body to the scene? The soul is then dragged by the body into the region of the changeable, and wanders and is confused; the world spins round her, and she is like a drunkard when under their influence?

The soul is cured of its maladies by certain incantations; these incantations are beautiful reasons, from which temperance is generated in souls.

The soul is in the very likeness of the divine, and immortal, and intelligible, and uniform, and indissoluble, and unchangeable; and the body is in the very likeness of the human, and mortal, and unintelligible, and multiform, and dissoluble, and changeable.

The soul is pure when it leaves the body and drags nothing bodily with it, by virtue of having no willing association with the body in life but avoiding it. Practicing philosophy in the right way is a training to die easily.

The soul then, as being immortal, and having been born again many times, and having seen all things that exist, whether in this world or in the world below, has knowledge of them all, all enquiry and all learning is but recollection.

The soul, being a harmony, can never utter a note at variance with the tensions and relaxations and vibrations and other affections of the strings out of which she is composed; she can only follow, she cannot lead them?...And yet do we not now discover the soul to be doing the exact opposite—leading the elements of which she is believed to be composed; almost always opposing and coercing them in all sorts of ways throughout life threatening and reprimanding the desires, passions, fears, as if talking to a thing which is not herself.

The soul, like the body, accepts by practice whatever habit one wishes it to contact.

The years wrinkle our skin, but lack of enthusiasm wrinkles our soul.

There are two kinds of disease of the soul, vice and ignorance.

All men's souls are immortal, but the souls of the righteous are immortal and divine.

Let us be careful of admitting into our souls the notion that there is no truth or health or soundness in any arguments at all; but let us rather say that there is as yet no health in us, and that we must quit ourselves like men and do our best to gain health— you and all other men with a view to the whole of your future life, and I myself with a view to death.

Spectator

Do you know that the spectator is the last of the rings which, as I am saying, receive the power of the original magnet from one another? The rhapsody like yourself and the actor are intermediate links, and the poet himself is the first of them. Through all these the God sways the souls of men in any direction which he pleases, and makes one man hang down from another. Thus there is a vast chain of dancers and masters and under masters of choruses, who are suspended, as if from the stone, at the side of the rings which hang down from the Muse.

My plainness of speech makes them hate me, and what is their hatred but a proof that I am speaking the truth.

Sphere

Do you suppose that I should have lived as long as I have if I had moved in the sphere of public life, and conducting myself in that sphere like an honourable man, had always upheld the cause of right, and conscientiously set this end above all other things? Not by a very long way, gentlemen; neither would any other man.

Spirit

The Spirit is neither good nor bad, it runs where the wild heart leads.

Will you not allow that I have as much of the spirit of prophecy in me as the swans? For they, when they perceive that they must die, having sung all their life long, do then sing more than ever, rejoicing in the thought that they are about to go away to the god whose ministers they are.

Strong

Strong minds discuss ideas, average minds discuss events, weak minds discuss people.

Success

The only place where success comes before work is in the dictionary. There is only one good, knowledge, and one evil, ignorance.

When you want success as badly as you want the air, then you will get it. There is no other secret of success.

If at first you don't succeed, avoid skydiving.

Suffer

If you don't get what you want, you suffer; if you get what you don't want, you suffer; even when you get exactly what you want, you still suffer because you can't hold on to it forever. Your mind is your predicament. It wants to be free of change. Free of pain, free of the obligations of life and death. But change is law and no amount of pretending will alter that reality.

It is never right to do wrong or to requite wrong with wrong, or when we suffer evil to defend ourselves by doing evil in return.

Sum

The sum of intelligence on the planet is a constant; the population is growing.

System

A system of morality which is based on relative emotional values is a mere illusion, a thoroughly vulgar conception which has nothing sound in it and nothing true.

Task

The hardest task needs the lightest hand or else its completion will not lead to freedom but to a tyranny much worse than the one it replaces.

Teach

I cannot teach anybody anything. I can only make them think.

No one can teach, if by teaching we mean the transmission of knowledge, in any mechanical fashion, from one person to another. The most that can be done is that one person who is more knowledgeable than another can, by asking a series of questions, stimulate the other to think, and so cause him to learn for himself.

Thank

Thank not those faithful who praise all thy words and actions; but those who kindly reprove thy faults.

Thing

All things in moderation, including moderation.

How many things are there which I do not want.

How many things I can do without!

How many things I have no need of!

How singular is the thing called pleasure, and how curiously related to pain, which might be thought to be the opposite of it; for they never come to a man together, and yet he who pursues either of them is generally compelled to take the other. They are two, and yet they grow together out of one head or stem.

I only know one thing, and that is I know nothing.

One thing I am ready to fight for as long as I can, in word and act: that is, that we shall be better, braver and more active men if we believe it right to look for what we don't know than if we believe there is no point in looking because what we don't know we can never discover.

One thing only I know, and that is that I know nothing'.

Think

We are what we think we are.

Thought

The highest realms of thought are impossible to reach without first attaining an understanding of compassion.

Travel

How can you wonder your travels do you no good, when you carry yourself around with you?

True

Is it true; is it kind, or is it necessary?

The true champion of justice, if he intends to survive even for a short time, must necessarily confine himself to private life and leave politics alone.

The true disciple of philosophy is likely to be misunderstood by other men; they do not perceive that he is ever pursuing death and dying; and if this is true, why, having had the desire of death all his life long, should he repine at that which he has always been pursuing and desiring?

True knowledge exists in knowing that you know nothing.

True knowledge exists in knowing that you know nothing. And in knowing that you know nothing, that makes you the smartest of all.

True perfection is a bold quest to seek. Only the willing and true of heart will seek the betterment of many.

True wisdom comes to each of us when we realize how little we understand about life, ourselves, and the world around us.

True wisdom lies in one's confession about the limits of one's knowledge.

Truth

We approach truth only inasmuch as we depart from life. For what do we, who love truth, strive after in life? To free ourselves from the body, and from all the evil that is caused by the life of the body! If so, then how can we fail to be glad when death comes to us?

Are you not ashamed of your eagerness to possess as much wealth, reputation, and honours as possible, while you do not care for nor give thought to wisdom or truth, or the best possible state of your soul?

I desire only to know the truth and to live as well as I can. And, to the utmost of my power, I exhort all other men to do the same. I exhort you also to take part in the great combat, which is the combat of life and greater than every other earthly conflict.

Lies are the greatest murder. They kill the Truth.

The first key to greatness is to be in reality what we appear to be.

The first sieve is the one of truth, did you examine what you were about to tell me if it is true? Socrates asks.

To them, I said, the truth would be literally nothing but the shadows of the images.

Understand

Tell me and i'll forget; show me and I may remember; involve me and i'll understand.

Understanding

Understanding a question is half an answer.

Universe

The unexamined c is not the life for man.

The unexamined life is not worth living for a human being.

The universe really is motion and nothing else.

This is a universe that does not favour the timid.

Use

To use words and phrases in an easygoing manner without scrutinizing them too curiously is not in general a mark of ill-breeding. On the contrary, there is something low-bred in being too precise. But sometimes there is no help for it.

Vanity

Through your rags I see your vanity.

Virtue

Virtue does not come from wealth, but wealth, and every other good thing which men have comes from virtue.

Virtue is the beauty of the soul.

Virtue is the nursing-mother of all human pleasures, who, in rendering them just, renders them also pure and permanent; in moderating them, keeps them in breath and appetite; in interdicting those which she herself refuses, whets our desires to those that she allows; and, like a kind and liberal mother, abundantly allows all that nature requires, even to satiety, if not to lassitude.

And so they grow richer and richer, and the more they think of making a fortune the less they think of virtue; for when riches and virtue are placed together in the scales of the balance, the one always rises as the other falls.

I do nothing but go about persuading you all, old and young alike, not to take thought for your persons or your properties, but and chiefly to care about the greatest improvement of the soul. I tell you that virtue is not given by money, but that from virtue comes money and every other good of man, public as well as private. This is my teaching, and if this is the doctrine which corrupts the youth, I am a mischievous person.

I sought to persuade every man among you that he must look to himself, and seek virtue and wisdom before he looks to his private interests, and look to the state before he looks to the interests of the state; and that this should be the order which he observes in all his actions.

There is a virtue, Simmias, which is named courage. Is not that a special attribute of the philosopher? Again, there is temperance.

Is not the calm, and control, and disdain of the passions which even the many call temperance, a quality belonging only to those who despise the body and live in philosophy?

Voluntarily

No one does wrong voluntarily.

Want

Those who want the fewest things are nearest to the gods.

Having the fewest wants, I am nearest to the gods.

If you want to be a good saddler, saddle the worst horse; for if you can take one, you can tame all.

If you want to be wrong then follow the masses.

If you want to know your own soul, you must talk to other people.

War

Wars and revolutions and battles are due simply and solely to the body and its desires. All wars are undertaken for the acquisition of wealth; and the reason why we have to acquire wealth is the body, because we are slaves in its service.

Way

The bad one is that way because of the ignorance, therefore he can be healed with wisdom.

The easiest and noblest way is not to be crushing others, but to be improving yourselves.

The right way to begin is to pay attention to the young, and make them just as good as possible.

The way to gain a good reputation, is to endeavour to be what you desire to appear.

Wealth

Wealth does not bring about excellence, but excellence brings about wealth and all other public and private blessings for men.

Wealth does not bring about excellence, but excellence makes wealth and everything else good for men, both individually and collectively.

Wealth does not bring goodness, but goodness brings wealth and every other blessing, both to the individual and to the state

All wars are fought for the acquisition of wealth.

Wheat

Nobody is qualified to become a statesman who is entirely ignorant of the problem of wheat.

Wind

The same wind is blowing, and yet one of us may be cold and the other not.

Wind buffs up empty bladders; opinion, fools.

Wisdom

Wisdom adorned riches and casted a shadow over poverty.

Wisdom begins in wonder.

All of the wisdom of this world is but a tiny raft upon which we must set sail when we leave this earth. If only there was a firmer foundation upon which to sail, perhaps some divine word.

For this fear of death is indeed the preteens of wisdom, and not real wisdom, being the appearance of knowing the unknown; since no one knows whether death, which they in their fear apprehend to be the greatest evil, may not be the greatest good.

I decided that it was not wisdom that enabled poets to write their poetry, but a kind of instinct or inspiration, such as you find in seers and prophets who deliver all their sublime messages without knowing in the least what they mean.

I realized that it was not by wisdom that poets write their poetry, but by a kind of nature or inspiration, such as you find in seers and prophets; for these also say many beautiful things, but do not know anything of what they say.

The definition of terms is the beginning of wisdom.

The only true wisdom is in knowing you know nothing.

The true Wisdom is in recognizing our own ignorance.

Those then who know not wisdom and virtue, and are always busy with gluttony and sensuality, go down and up again as far as the mean; and in this region they move at random throughout life, but they never pass into the true upper world; thither they neither look, nor do they ever find their way, neither are they truly filled with true being, nor do they ever taste of pure and abiding pleasure.

When you want wisdom and insight as badly as you want to breathe, it is then you shall have it.

By far the greatest and most admirable form of wisdom is that needed to plan and beautify cities and human communities.

Wise

I am called wise, for my hearers always imagine that I myself possess wisdom which I find wanting in others: but the truth is, O men of Athens, that God only is wise; and in this oracle he means to say that the wisdom of men is little or nothing. As if he said, He, O men, is the wisest, who like Socrates, knows that his wisdom is in truth worth nothing. And so I go on my way, obedient to the god, and make inquisition into anyone, whether citizen or stranger, who appears to be wise; and if he is not wise, then in vindication of the oracle I show him that he is not wise; and this occupation quite absorbs me, and I have no time to give either to any public matter of interest or to any concern of my own, but I am in utter poverty by reason of my devotion to the god.

I am likely to be wiser than he to this small, extent, that I do not think I know what I do not know.

I am very conscious that I am not wise at all.

I am wiser than this man, for neither of us appears to know anything great and good; but he fancies he knows something, although he knows nothing; whereas I, as I do not know anything, so I do not fancy I do. In this trifling particular, then, I appear to be wiser than he, because I do not fancy I know what I do not know.

I'm wiser than that person. For it's likely that neither of us knows anything fine and good, but he thinks he knows something he doesn't know, whereas I, since I don't in fact know, don't think that I do either. At any rate, it seems that I'm wiser than he in just this one small way: that what I don't know, I don't think I know.

So I withdrew and thought to myself: 'I am wiser than this man; it is likely that neither of us knows anything worthwhile, but he thinks he knows something when he does not, whereas when I do not know, neither do I think I know; so I am likely to be wiser than he to this small extent, that I do not think I know what I do not know.

The wise man seeks death all his life, and for this reason death is not terrifying to him.

Well I am certainly wiser than this man. It is only too likely that neither of us has any knowledge to boast of; but he thinks that he knows something which he does not know, whereas I am quite conscious of my ignorance. At any rate it seems that I am wiser than he is to this small extent, that I do not think that I know what I do not know.

When I left him, I reasoned thus with myself: I am wiser than this man, for neither of us appears to know anything great and good; but he fancies he knows something, although he knows nothing; whereas I, as I do not know anything, so I do not fancy I do. In this trifling particular, then, I appear to be wiser than he, because I do not fancy I know what I do not know.

Woman

Trust not a woman when she weeps, for it is her nature to weep when she wants her will.

When a woman is allowed to become a man's equal, she becomes his superior.

Wonder

Why do you wonder that globetrotting does not help you, seeing that you always take yourself with you? The reason that set you wandering is ever at your heels.

Wonder is the beginning of wisdom.

Wonder is the feeling of a philosopher, and philosophy begins in wonder.

This sense of wonder is the mark of the philosopher. Philosophy indeed has no other origin.

World

The rest of the world lives to eat, while I eat to live.

Wrong

Since I am convinced that I wrong no one, I am not likely to wrong myself.

Yield

I will not yield to any man contrary to what is right, for fear of death, even if I should die at once for not yielding.

Young

The young people of today think of nothing but themselves. They have no reverence for parents or old age. They are impatient of all restraint. They talk as if they alone knew everything and what passes for wisdom with us is foolishness with them. As for girls, they are forward, immodest and unwomanly in speech, behaviour and dress.

What is happening to our young people? They disrespect their elders, they disobey their parents. They ignore the law. They riot in the streets inflamed with wild notions. Their morals are decaying. What is to become of them?

When I was young, Cebes, I had a prodigious desire to know the department of philosophy which is called Natural Science; this appeared to me to have lofty aims, as being the science which has to do with the causes of things, and which teaches why a thing is, and is created and destroyed; and I always agitated myself with the consideration of such questions as these...I went on to examine the decay of them, and then to the study of the heaven and earth, and at last I concluded that I was wholly incapable of these inquiries... There was a time when I thought that I understood the meaning of greater and less pretty well... That ten is more than eight, and that two cubits are more than one, because two is twice one. I should be far from imagining... That I knew the cause of any of them, indeed I should, for I cannot satisfy myself that when one is added to one, the one to which the addition is made becomes two...nor can I understand how the division of one is the way to make two; for then a different cause would produce the same effect.

When I was young, I believed that life might unfold in an orderly way, according to my hopes and expectations. But now I understand that the Way winds like a river, always changing, ever onward.. My journeys revealed that the Way itself creates the warrior; that every path leads to peace, every choice to wisdom. And that life has always been, and will always be, arising in Mystery.

Young men of the richer classes, who have not much to do, come about me of their own accord; they like to hear the pretenders examined, and they often imitate me, and proceed to examine others; there are plenty of persons, as they quickly discover, who think that they know something, but really know little or nothing; and then those who are examined by them instead of being angry with themselves are angry with me: This confounded Socrates, they say; this villainous misleaders of youth! And then if somebody asks them, Why, what evil does he practice or teach? They do not know, and cannot tell; but in order that they may not appear to be at a loss, they repeat the ready-made charges which are used against all philosophers about teaching things up in the clouds and under the earth, and having no gods, and making the worse appear the better cause; for they do not like to confess that their pretence of knowledge has been detected which is the truth; and as they are numerous and ambitious and energetic, and are drawn up in battle array and have persuasive tongues, they have filled your ears with their loud and inveterate calumnies.

Young people nowadays love luxury; they have bad manners and contempt for authority. They show disrespect for old people contradict their parents, talk constantly in front of company, gobble their food and tyrannize their teachers.

Youth

For I do nothing but go about persuading you all, old and young alike, not to take thought for your persons or your properties, but for the highest welfare of your souls, proclaiming as I go, 'Wealth does not bring goodness, but goodness brings wealth and every other blessing, both to the individual and to the State.' This is my teaching, and if this is the doctrine which corrupts the youth, I am a mischievous person. But if any one says that this is not my teaching, he is speaking an untruth.

If the whole world depends on today's youth, I can't see the world lasting another 100 years.

In childhood be modest, in youth temperate, in adulthood just, and in old age prudent.

Zeus

I swear it upon Zeus an outstanding runner cannot be the equal of an average wrestler.

□

References

1. www.simplelifestrategies.com/
2. www.quotationspage.com/
3. www.ranker.com/
4. www.lifehack.org/
5. www.en.wikiquote.org
6. www.en.proverbia.net/
7. www.quotes.net/
8. www.goodreads.com
9. www.brainyquote.com/

❑❑❑